P9-CRQ-334

IS COLLEGE WORTH IT?

IS COLLEGE WORTH IT?

A FORMER UNITED STATES SECRETARY OF EDUCATION AND A LIBERAL ARTS GRADUATE EXPOSE THE BROKEN PROMISE OF HIGHER EDUCATION

WILLIAM J. BENNETT
AND DAVID WILEZOL

THOMAS NELSON
Since 1798

NASHVILLE DALLAS MEXICO CITY RIO DE JANEIRO

Published in Nashville, Tennessee, by Thomas Nelson. Thomas Nelson is a registered trademark of Thomas Nelson, Inc.

Thomas Nelson, Inc., titles may be purchased in bulk for educational, business, fund-raising, or sales promotional use. For information, please e-mail SpecialMarkets@ThomasNelson.com.

ISBN 978-1-59555-279-2
ISBN 978-1-59555-422-2 (eBook)

Library of Congress Control Number: 2013931897

Printed in the United States of America

13 14 15 16 17 RRD 6 5 4 3 2 1

Contents

The Truth about College

- Two-thirds of people who go to four-year colleges right out of high school should do something else.
- A character in *Good Will Hunting* was right: "In fifty years . . . you're going to come up with the fact that . . . you dropped one hundred and fifty grand on [an] . . . education that you could have got for a dollar fifty in late charges at the public library!"[1] Students pay $100,000 or more for what they could get for almost nothing. With new technology and online breakthroughs, you could get a better education in a coffee shop or your parents' basement than you will get at most colleges.
- If you are accepted into the Colorado School of Mines, Harvey Mudd, Stanford, Plan II at the University of Texas, and dozens of other places (see chapter 3), then go. And if you want to study petroleum engineering or any kind of engineering and have an aptitude for it, then go.

- If you don't know why you're going to college or if you're going mainly because most everyone you know goes, don't go, or at least wait and better assess the merits of going.
- Half of all college graduates in 2010–11 were unemployed or dramatically underemployed.[2]
- People are putting off or even giving up on their life dreams because of college debt. The price and cost of college are frighteningly high.
- Upon graduation, a college degree today is more likely to guarantee you debt than a well-paying job.
- In today's colleges, much of what is taught in the humanities and social sciences is nonsense (or nonsense on stilts), politically tendentious, and worth little in the marketplace and for the enrichment of your mind or soul.
- Arguably the three most successful college attendees of our generation were dropouts—Steve Jobs, Bill Gates, and Mark Zuckerberg.
- By the year 2018, nearly fourteen million jobs will be available that will require more than a high school diploma but less than a BA.[3]
- Eighty-four percent of employers rate college graduates as unprepared or only somewhat prepared for the job.[4]
- If all of K–12 education in the United States were as good as the best of K–12 education in the United States, America's high school graduates would be better educated than most of today's college graduates.

- College costs and prices rise and will continue to rise far above the rate of inflation (as has been the case for decades) because (a) many colleges are greedy, (b) families will pay anything to get their kids into some colleges, and (c) the federal government endlessly subsidizes these increases.
- It is commonly said that the difference between a high school diploma and a college degree is $1 million in lifetime earnings. But it is likely that most of those assets are found in the banks of the graduates of the top 150 universities and colleges. For most college graduates, once subtracting the cost of their college education, the difference between what they will earn and what a similarly talented and motivated high school graduate will earn is much less.
- Whether the standard of excellence for higher education is cultivating the mind and the soul or maximizing financial return on investment, most of higher education fails most students.

INTRODUCTION

The American system of higher education comprises some of the best universities, professors, and students the world has ever seen. Over time, having a college degree has become synonymous with success. It has long been considered the path to a better, higher-paying job; the best way to make connections and propel a career; and a status symbol—especially for those who go to elite universities. These are deeply ingrained ideas, and millions of students in America and around the globe want nothing more than to attend an American university. For many students there are still strong reasons to go to college, but not so for all who go. Many of America's colleges and universities today have serious academic, institutional, and other performance problems, and they are quickly approaching a crisis point, if they are not there already. Too much of higher education is wildly expensive. Tuition costs are at all-time highs and rising, and in turn, so are student-loan debts and student-loan defaults. Total student-loan debt in the United States has surpassed $1 trillion, and there are legitimate fears that it could be the next economic bubble to burst, crushing millions of low-income and middle-class students.[1]

The warning signs are everywhere. Recent data from

the Census Bureau and Department of Labor found that almost 54 percent of recent graduates were unemployed or underemployed.[2] In many cases, a college diploma no longer guarantees the high potential lifetime earnings it once did. On top of that, students often graduate having learned little, or they don't graduate at all. Millions of skilled jobs worldwide are going unfilled because of a lack of trained, educated workers. With a few exceptions, academic standards and performance at universities and colleges are slipping, while costs and debt continue to increase.

Still, this hasn't stopped an overwhelming number of students from paying an exorbitant amount of money or taking on huge amounts of debt in order to attend college. Families will go to incredible—and sometimes insane—lengths to get their sons or daughters into college.

At too many colleges and universities, there is an immense gap between a student's or parent's investment and the return on investment (ROI). There is no one culprit at fault. The problems have metastasized at many levels, including

- the federal government's role in student aid,
- the accountability and transparency of the universities and colleges,
- poorly performing high schools, and
- uninformed consumers (both students and their parents).

At the core of these problems is the commonly held belief that "everyone should go to college." But why? The truth is that too many people are going to college. Too many students are studying irrelevant material that leaves them ill equipped for the job market. Too many students are paying too much for tuition and are left holding massive amounts of debt. Too many students are going to college and doing little other than indulging their own pastimes, partying, and hooking up.

College, as currently apprised, should not be a universal commodity. As the K–12 experience concludes, each young man or woman should do a serious self-evaluation with the help of others and then chart an appropriate postsecondary course. Doing this is wiser than blindly presupposing that college is a necessary good. Each student and parent must critically evaluate the data: student-loan debt, return on investment, lifetime salary earnings, academic performance, skills training, the student's abilities and interests, and so on. Rather than simply swallowing the conventional wisdom and following the conventional path, more students need to make realistic assessments of their abilities and finances and then decide the best path for their lives.

For example, as the stories and facts in this book show, if you get into Stanford, no matter what you study, you should probably go. The average lifetime earnings of a Stanford graduate will probably far exceed any debt he or she might shoulder. Also, if you are interested in petroleum engineering and have an aptitude for it, you should go to a college with a good petroleum engineering program. Petroleum engineering is ranked as the top salary-grossing major by midcareer earnings, pulling in well over six figures (see chapter 3). However, if you get into a middling or poorly performing private university and take on high five- or six-figure debts to major in an obscure field like medieval studies or anthropology, you should probably *not* go—or you should at least be fully aware of your high risk of long-term debt and low chances of gainful employment.

College should be a choice for some, depending on educational prowess, opportunity, and financial considerations. For those individuals, only a certain number of colleges are appropriate, and of those colleges, only a few degrees are worth choosing. College is neither a panacea nor a carte blanche. Better high schools, trade schools, and apprenticeship programs should take the place of overpriced and underperforming colleges and universities. Online education, particularly MOOCs (massive open online courses), should take the place of inefficient brick-and-mortar colleges, making education of all types less expensive and more accessible.

Critics may argue that we are trying to discourage low-income and middle-class students from pursuing success and we are looking out for the interests of only the rich, elite, or most talented students. That couldn't be further from the truth. The world's most talented students will be successful no matter where they go to college or if they don't go at all. They can also bear the brunt of expensive tuition, student loans, and poor employment prospects. The vast majority of students below them, financially and academically, cannot. The financial pain and burden of student loan debt and post-secondary unemployment falls on many, but it falls harder on the poor and underprivileged. A failing higher education system stunts their upward mobility more than anyone else's. It is out of concern for the vast majority of these students that we penned this book.

Chapter 1 examines the scope of higher education's

financial crisis and how society's frequently wrong conceptions of higher education are adding fuel to the fire. The amount of student-loan debt weighing down our economy and its future workers will shock you. Like the subprime mortgage crisis in the late 2000s, student-loan debt may be the next bubble to burst.

How then do we rein in rising tuition costs and student-loan debt? Chapter 2 answers those questions. By exposing how and why ill-advised policies on the part of the government and schools alike have created this national student debt crisis, we offer solutions to make college more affordable and save future generations from crushing debt.

With high risk of debt and underemployment, how do you know which college or university is worth your investment? Chapter 3 analyzes the many factors that make a college education worth the price—or not. Using this analysis, we offer our unique lists of the best majors and colleges and universities for people looking to maximize their financial returns and avoid debt. You will be surprised by the schools that make our lists and those that don't.

But higher education isn't solely about financial returns; the first duty of any school is education. Chapter 4 exposes the frighteningly paltry amount of learning taking place on some college campuses. And, for the exorbitant prices that students and parents pay for a college education, too many of our students are not being equipped to be competitive in the global workforce.

Chapter 5 proposes our solutions and recommendations for the various problems in higher education, and how online learning is leading a revolution to reshape higher education and make it more affordable and accessible for everyone.

There are multiple purposes of higher education: to educate and equip the mind and the soul to recognize what is right and good in life, to prepare a student for the demands of a modern labor market, and to offer specialized learning in various fields and occupations. Whether you believe a college education should be thought of as a good in itself or job training or concentrated specialized learning—or a combination of all three—this book demonstrates how higher education is failing on multiple fronts.

It's time for parents and students to look at the entire enterprise of higher education and ask how, when, where, for whom, in what studies, and at what cost is a college education appropriate? And if it is not appropriate, what are the alternatives?

We're not saying, "Don't go to college." We're saying, "Maybe you should go. It all depends. But if you go, go with your eyes wide-open."

ONE

The Borrowing Binge

In the mid-1980s, at age thirty-nine, Carol Todd began borrowing money from the federal government and private lenders to attend college. She first pursued a GED, then an associate's degree, and then a bachelor's degree from two private colleges—all paid for with student loans.

She went on to earn two master's degrees from Towson State University in Maryland. In 1992, she entered the University of Baltimore School of Law, but she didn't graduate. After a lengthy hiatus from school she decided that her education was still incomplete. So in 2007 she earned a PhD from an online, unaccredited university.

Todd had borrowed her way through twenty years of higher education, taking advantage of every benefit that government lenders, private lenders, and colleges and universities would offer. And she racked up an astonishing $339,361 in student-loan debts.

There was no way she could possibly pay it back. And she doesn't have to. On May 17, 2012, a US bankruptcy judge ruled that Todd, by this time sixty-five, had the right to discharge her loans.[1]

Todd had met the famously stringent "undue hardship" exemption. Her excuse? Asperger's syndrome, an autism spectrum disorder (ASD) that often makes social interaction difficult and can be characterized by repetitive patterns of behavior and interests.

One could certainly question the legitimacy and justice of such a ruling. How debilitating is her condition, after all, considering she successfully completed hundreds of credit hours of academic work?

But the real question is, how was Todd allowed to borrow so much money over so much time when she never demonstrated an ability to repay it? Why didn't anyone ever stop and question Todd's creditworthiness? Who is on the hook for all of her unpaid loans?

Zombie Generation

Todd has an extreme amount of debt, but her story, as it relates to student-loan obligations and problematic lending policies, is not so unusual. Many of today's college graduates are suffocating under mountains of debt, with slim chances of gaining suitable employment to pay back their debt in a timely manner.

At a beachside restaurant in North Carolina last spring, we struck up a conversation with a thirty-four-year-old bartender. In between fixing cocktails, he grimly told us that when he graduated from college, he had accumulated more than $50,000 in debt. He still had about $40,000 left to pay and felt disillusioned with his prospects of ever paying it back. "I didn't go to college to have this job," he said with a sigh. "I'm living in a box." It was hard to tell whether this was a comment on his living arrangements or prospects in life.[2]

For too many college students this story is becoming the norm. "We are creating a zombie generation of young people, larded with debt, and, in many cases dropouts without any diploma," said Mark Zandi, chief economist at Moody's, the credit-ratings giant.[3]

A *New York Times* series profiled several graduates in their struggle to dig out from their massive school loans. One young woman, a graduate of Ohio Northern University, is currently carrying a debt load of $120,000 and works at two restaurants while searching for a full-time job in marketing. Another, a dropout from Bowling Green University, works three jobs to pay down her $70,000 debt. "I'll be paying this forever," she says. She doesn't even entertain the idea of going back to school someday: "For me to finish it would mean borrowing more money. It makes me puke to think about borrowing more money."[4]

According to the National Center for Education Statistics' National Postsecondary Student Aid Study, 53 percent of all full-time students took out student loans in 2007–8, the last year for which data are available.[5] The average debt load per student upon graduation now runs $23,300, according to the Federal Reserve. About 25 percent of borrowers owe more than $28,000, whereas 10 percent owe more than $54,000,

3.1 percent owe more than $100,000, and 0.45 percent owe more than $200,000.[6] (In 2007, there were approximately 11.3 million full-time students, which means that more than 50,000 borrowers owe more than $200,000—not an insignificant number.)

Considering there are approximately twelve million full-time postsecondary students in the United States, this debt is spread far and wide across the US economy.[7] In fact, the Pew Research firm conducted a survey in September 2012, showing that one in every five households in the nation owed student-loan debt. Forty percent of households headed by someone under age thirty-five owe student-loan debt.[8]

Mark Kantrowitz, who runs FinAid.org, one of the leading websites devoted to helping students understand the cost of higher education, estimated that in late 2011, the nation's combined federal and private student-loan debt surpassed $1 trillion, and that the nation's student-loan debt continues to increase at a rate of $2,853.88 *per second*.[9] June 2010 marked the first time that Americans' total student-loan debt surpassed their total credit card debt.[10] Clearly, educational debt isn't a small phenomenon.

Expecting, and subsequently acquiring, some burden of student-loan debt is now the norm for people considering college, even before enrollment begins. More than half of college freshmen expected to cover at least some of their education through student loans, according to a 2010 survey conducted by the *Chronicle of Higher Education*.[11] The pervasiveness of student debt has seeped so far into the culture that in one episode of the *Simpsons*, after busting open the cash register of the hapless bartender Moe, the bandit declares, "Good-bye student loan payments!" Not exactly what John Dillinger would have done with his haul. Even President Barack Obama took out student loans and told a crowd of students in 2012, "We [Michelle and I] only finished paying our student loans off eight years ago."[12]

Although the burden of student-loan debt has typically been associated with those in their twenties, it is quickly becoming a cross-generational problem. According to the Federal Reserve, those between thirty and thirty-nine owe more than any other age group, with a per-borrower debt load of $28,500, and they're followed by borrowers between the ages of forty and forty-nine, who had an average of $26,000.[13]

Peter Morici, an economics professor at the University of Maryland, highlighted the lifetime cost of a college education in an interview with the Catholic News Service, saying, "More than 15 percent [of debtors] are still paying back student loans at age 50. They should have long ago been retired. We have folks that are being hounded by collection agencies in their 80s. We've got Social Security checks being garnished."[14] Contributing to these hardships is the fact that, unlike a mortgage or a business debt, student-loan debts can never be discharged in bankruptcy. If you default (defined as nine consecutive missed payments), you can expect harassment from collection agencies and wage garnishment until you can voluntarily make payments again, except in cases where extreme hardship or disability can be proven, like Carol Todd's.

For some, the debt crisis has absurd and disturbing consequences. One *Huffington Post* article profiled a series of New York women who made "Sugar Daddy" arrangements—having sex with wealthy, usually aging New York men for money to pay off tuition, rent, or most commonly, student-loan debt. "I guess what finally pushed me over the edge was that I needed help to pay off my loans from school," said one twenty-five-year-old student. She added, "If this isn't what prostitution is called, I don't know what is." Hundreds of women purporting to be either current or former NYU and Harvard students were listed on one website devoted to such arrangements.[15]

Constants Are Changing

Compounding the debt crisis even more, these mountains of debt are being piled onto the shoulders of an already weak economy. Students have hitherto considered a college education to be a talisman against economic hardship, and they've assumed that they will be able to pay down all their debt with workplace earnings.[16] But since the recession of 2008, students are not seeing the anticipated high return (good jobs) on their pricey investment (high debt). One graduate who hoped his major in political science would help him find a job with the government is currently unemployed and sitting on $100,000 in debt. "Was college worth getting in the amount of debt I'm in? . . . At this point, I can't answer that."[17]

One unemployed grad who "powered through my four

years of college with the assumption that doing well and getting my bachelor's degree would be the key to having a future" talked to a writer for the *New York Times* about his frustration:

> I will be brutally honest, my post-graduation experience has turned from hopeful to bitter very quickly. . . . I graduated with a 3.76 G.P.A. and was inducted into Phi Beta Kappa. I joined the student council. I spent four summers interning for the Fresh Air Fund and volunteered for the Alzheimer's Association. I have nothing to show for my hard work but $24,000 in student loans. I've lost count of the number of job applications that have been ignored, and the ones that I did receive a response to still sting. I've stopped carrying both the house phone and my cellphone with me to every room that I move to, and I've stopped checking my e-mail every 20 minutes. I'm still trying because I have no other choice.[18]

Columnist Frank Bruni, writing for the *New York Times*, put the larger post-college and unemployed ennui this way:

> For a long time and for a lot of us, "college" was more or less a synonym for success. We had only to go. We had only to graduate. And if we did, according to parents and high-school guidance counselors and everything we heard and everything we read, we could pretty much count on a career, just about depend on a decent income and more or less expect security. *A diploma wasn't a piece of paper. It was an amulet.*[19]

But as the economy recessed in 2008, and still continues to languish, the calculation that college is worth its high cost is looking like much less of a sure thing. The employment prospects of recent graduates are abysmal. One Associated Press analysis of data on 2011 graduates found that 54 percent of recent graduates were unemployed.[20] And many of those who were employed found themselves in jobs that didn't require anything to do with their degree—often service jobs like waiting tables or working at retail stores. That fact helps explain the findings of a Rutgers University study that pegged the median starting salary for students graduating from four-year colleges in 2009 and 2010 at $27,000, down from $30,000 for those who entered the work force from 2006 to 2008.[21]

Mark Cuban, entrepreneur and owner of the NBA's Dallas Mavericks, has analogized America's pursuit of a college education to the grab for real estate that characterized the subprime-mortgage crisis:

> Right now there is a never ending supply of buyers. Students who can't get jobs or who think that by going to college they enhance their chances to get a job. It's the collegiate equivalent of flipping houses. You borrow as much money as you can for the best school you can get into and afford and then you "flip" that education for the great job you are going to get when you graduate.
>
> Except those great jobs aren't always there.[22]

Perceiving their long-term economic prospects to be dimming and their debt bills mounting, many of those who have sizable loans or who can't find work (or both) are doubling down on higher education and investing in graduate degrees. They are calculating that, despite the high cost, this, too, will produce a substantial return on investment, at least one big enough to pay down debt and live comfortably.

In the long run, almost all studies have shown an earnings premium on postgraduate education, but with these higher earnings come higher debts. The costs of graduate school are often as much as or equal to an undergrad education. The median amount of debt for an MA is about $25,000, a PhD $52,000, and a professional degree around $80,000.[23] Law students routinely graduate with $150,000 of debt for a JD, and in many cases that's on top of undergrad debt. Like many undergraduates, graduate students have spent additional tens of thousands of dollars on a graduate degree that has not produced the returns anticipated. Jobs are scarce for many with postgraduate education. The *Chronicle of Higher Education* found that the number of PhDs on food stamps tripled between 2007 and 2010.[24]

This problem of mounting debt from graduate school is particularly acute in the humanities. The *Chronicle* interviewed one woman, a forty-three-year-old single mother with a PhD in medieval studies. She receives food stamps and Medicare, despite her adjunct position at an Arizona college. "I am not a welfare queen," she said. "I find it horrifying that someone who stands in front of college classes and teaches is on welfare." The *Chronicle* also profiled an adjunct professor of film studies currently writing his dissertation. He and his family have accepted public assistance for the last few years while struggling to make ends meet. "Living on the dole is excruciatingly embarrassing and a constant reminder that I must have done something terribly wrong along the way to deserve this fate," he agonized.[25] Fordham University professor Leonard Cassuto hit the nail on the head when he described many graduate students as "intellectual sharecroppers."[26] Many devotees of the liberal arts who have chosen to follow their dreams of obtaining a decent paying professorship are currently languishing at near poverty levels.

Even those getting law degrees—long thought to be a guarantee of job security—have been affected by the economic malaise. Only 55 percent of law school graduates in 2011 had full-time, long-term positions requiring a law degree nine months after graduation, according to an analysis by the *Wall Street Journal*. Shockingly, "only about 8% of 2011 graduates landed full-time, long-term jobs at larger firms with more than 250 attorneys," the *Journal* reported. The problem does not seem likely to abate anytime soon.[27] The Bureau of Labor Statistics forecasted only about 72,000 full-time lawyer jobs opening in the remainder of this decade, for an estimated 300,000 law school graduates in that time span.[28]

From top to bottom, from graduate to undergraduate, very few students have been immune to the student-debt debacle, and the economic crisis has only exaggerated it.

The College Craze

This recent glut of qualified degree holders competing for a dearth of jobs can to some extent be ascribed to the recession of 2008. But there's a good chance that America has over-bought into the idea of college for everyone—a view that has grown since the 1980s. About a year after graduation, according to the Bureau of Labor Statistics, 68 percent of 2011 high school graduates were enrolled in college, 91 percent of them as full-time students.[29]

For many graduating high school students and their parents, college is now "the default activity," in the words of billionaire venture capitalist and educational trailblazer Peter Thiel.[30] He delivered his point with a critical tone. To him, many Americans are enrolling in college without exploring their motivations for exactly why they are doing so.

Dr. Charles Murray, a friend and colleague of ours, has put the matter succinctly in his article, "What's Wrong With Vocational School?" Murray, echoing Thiel, theorizes that high school grads attend college in such large numbers "because their parents are paying for it and college is what children of the social class are supposed to do after they finish high school."[31] It's not needed so much as expected. Skipping college is a mark of failure, not merely a determination to walk another, perhaps better-suited road.

Indeed, our culture pushes college more than any other life path. Virtually every high school in America has a form of college preparatory instruction. Parents hammer home the importance of good grades in high school to get into a good college, though the motivation for students might be different from that of their parents. Movies like *Old School, Van Wilder*, and *Slackers* perpetuate the idea that college is primarily an adult playground with easy access to booze, drugs, sex, and mischief. Tom Wolfe chronicled this in his novel *I Am Charlotte Simmons.* We will see in a later chapter that much of the modern stereotype of college is true: students are doing far less work and wasting far more time than their predecessors. As the idea of college as the default activity has grown, the idea that shouldering debt to pay for it has become the norm. US secretary of education Arne Duncan expressed the prevailing orthodoxy on educational debt in 2012, saying that "when that debt is manageable . . . this is not bad debt to have."[32] Since most grads have been able to pay down their debt, Duncan is generally right. Enduring short-term sacrifices for a long-term payoff is central to the American work ethic. But some decisions to take on debt, partly because it is a cultural norm, are badly misguided. One young woman with $80,000 in debt admitted to the *New York Times* that the ubiquity of student loans was a justification for her to go into debt too. "The overall message was, 'It's doable and normal to go into that much debt,'" she said.[33] This is apparently the only circumstance in which parents agree that because "everyone else is doing it," it must be a good idea for their child too.

Student borrowing, at least in the last decade or so, can also perhaps be explained by the uniquely optimistic approach to life of the millennial generation, those born from the early 1980s and onward. Borrowing money is a fairly risky practice, as are all presumptions upon the future, but students have shown no sign toward slowing down. Ninety percent characterize their school debt as "an investment in the future."[34] This comfort with debt indicates a blithe (and perhaps delusional) hope that everything will work out, despite few real reasons for such a hope. Over the last decade, Pew Research did a series of studies on millennials that highlighted their unique attitudes, compared to other generations. Two years before the 2008 recession, 87 percent of unemployed millennials agreed that they "don't have enough income now but will in the future."[35] Remarkably, when asked the same question in 2010, 89 percent of millennials agreed with the statement, despite *worse* economic prospects. The young have always had a rosier outlook, which is always good and needed, but millennial optimism might need to be more realistic given the circumstances.

What Are We Paying?

The first and most direct connection to runaway student-loan debt is tuition cost. Student loans are tied to tuition costs, just as mortgages are tied to home prices. As tuition costs rise, students borrow more to finance their educations. But there is a vicious cycle here. History shows that as student-loan borrowing increases, there is a parallel and simultaneous increase in tuition costs.

Let's examine the trends.

According to the US Department of Education, for the 2010–11 academic year, annual prices for undergraduate tuition, room, and board were estimated to be $13,297 at public institutions and $31,395 at private institutions. Adjusting for inflation, those numbers are up 42 percent for public institutions and 19 percent for private institutions from the prior decade.[36] Barron's reported in April 2012 that since 1990, the price of tuition at four-year schools has soared 300 percent, four times the rate of inflation.[37] If trends continue through 2016, according to the Department of Education, the average cost of attending a public college will have more than doubled in just fifteen years.[38] The *Chronicle of Higher Education* reported in November 2011 that 123 American four-year colleges are now charging more than $50,000 per year for tuition, fees, room, and board.[39] With this in mind, even $32,000 per year for private college can start to look like a deal.

Furthermore, the costs don't seem to be receding anytime soon. In 2011 alone, costs at the average public university rose 5.4 percent for in-state students, or about $1,100. Average tuition at public universities rose 8.3 percent. The increases have greatly outpaced the rate of inflation, which was 3 percent in 2011.[40]

The price hikes at public institutions are particularly troubling because that is where the large majority of American students receive a college education. Take the state of Alabama for example. On a list of state economies ranked by gross domestic product (GDP), Alabama typically falls smack in the middle of the pack. But undergraduate tuition costs for in-state students at four-year public Alabama universities have exploded 172.4 percent since 2000. At the University of Alabama and Auburn University—two of the country's most renowned public universities—tuition fees have risen even faster. In 2000, Alabama's in-state tuition rate was $3,014 per year. In 2012 it was $9,200, an increase of 205.2 percent. During the same period at Auburn, tuition fees rose from $3,154 to $9,446, an increase of 199.4 percent.[41] Students at the top end of the education spectrum—private universities or graduate schools—have certainly felt the financial squeeze of higher tuition rates; but on average, they are better equipped financially and academically to handle the higher costs. The large majority of American students attending four-year public institutions are not, and they are the students most likely to default on their loans or not graduate from college.

And How Are We Paying For It?

With costs of college rising faster than ever, how are students financing it in the first place?

The College Board calculates that in 2011–12, more than $236 billion in financial aid was given to undergraduates and graduates in the forms of grants, federal loans, work study programs, and tax credits and deductions. Another $8 billion was borrowed from private, state, and institutional institutions. Of that $236 billion the total amount of education loans was $113.4 billion, which has more than doubled from $55.7 billion in 2001–02.

While the amount of financial aid has increased dramatically, families continue to bear a large burden of college funding, and we know that their wages are certainly not rising at anywhere near the same rate as the cost of college. Sallie Mae, a massive student-loan lender, reported that 30 percent of all college costs were covered by family income in 2011.[42] Families are clearly prioritizing saving and paying for a college education, but they are making sacrifices to do so. Sallie Mae noted that the average middle-class family paid $6,300 per year out of its own income and savings for a student's education.[43] Families must make sacrifices to afford college, particularly in tough economic times. We know they are driving beat-up cars, working two jobs, and cutting back on entertainment or dining out. On my (Bill's) radio show, *Morning in America*, I routinely talk to Jeff, a dad in Colorado Springs who works a day job and then drives a taxicab at night to be able to pay for his daughter's college education and keep her out of debt. We honor those who forego their own comfort to give their children a better-educated and economically prosperous future, one often better than they themselves have had. It is especially disconcerting when the quality of education they are sacrificing to purchase is poor. (More on that in a later chapter.)

Fortunately for students and their parents, according to Sallie Mae, one in three dollars spent on college education came from grants and scholarships.[44] The ubiquity of financial assistance bespeaks a larger problem with the cost of college, and even drives up the cost of tuition in many cases, but in the short run it helps many students and families finance part of their educations.

Tellingly, Sallie Mae found that only 11 percent of all college costs are paid for by students' own income and savings.[45] This is a major departure from earlier days when students were able to save up enough money on summer break to pay for next year's tuition, leaving them no or little debt. More than 1,400 readers commented on a particular *New York Times* article about the student debt crisis. One commenter, from Kansas City, Kansas, recounted his experience paying for college in the 1970s:

> In 1974, my tuition bill at the University of Kansas was $128.00/semester. Books were about $50.00 a semester, and there was a student activity fee of around $30.00. My dormitory fees (including 20 meals per week) were around $900.00 for the academic year. I was able to pay for my first year of college by pumping gas (remember that?) and doing light mechanical work for tips during the summer. I made $3.50 an hour, which was about two-and-a-half times the minimum wage. I did earn some overtime, but not enough to feel overwhelmed. I had plenty of goof-off time that summer, as I recall.[46]

Although some college students work a part-time or full-time job to cover the costs of their education, this is a very rare occurrence these days. Few can save $5,000, $10,000, or $20,000 in a summer waiting tables or working as a lifeguard.

Over the course of the twentieth century, college became as American as apple pie largely because it was affordable and because future earnings exceeded the tuition costs. Today, that's no longer true for many students and their families. Students are mortgaging their futures to finance their educations, but they cannot sell or leverage their diplomas as one could deal with a home mortgage. Instead, they are diverting current and future income to their education with the hope that they will one day recoup their spending with higher future earnings; but that is no longer guaranteed. The public is beginning to wake up, however. According to a recent poll by Country Financial and Rasmussen Reports, 57 percent of adults think college is a worthwhile investment. In 2008, the number was 81 percent.[47]

The Unseen Costs

The problem of huge student-loan debts is not just a burden on individuals. The consequences extend into numerous areas of society. With more money being pumped into debt repayment rather than the economy, debts are becoming a long-term drag on graduates' abilities to get ahead in life.

According to one survey of recent college graduates conducted by Rutgers University, 40 percent of them had delayed making a major purchase, such as a home or a car, because of college debt. Twenty-five percent had put off continuing their educations or moved in with relatives to save money.[48] One heartbreaking piece in the *Wall Street Journal* profiled a twenty-six-year-old with $74,000 in debt just from her BA, who pays 60 percent of her income to her loans. Her fiancé, age thirty-one, devotes 40 percent of his income to the same purpose. They can't afford to buy a house or travel to visit their families.[49] Another thirty-two-year-old woman carrying $98,000 of debt lamented that she and her husband can't even entertain the prospect of family. "How could I consider having children if I can barely support myself?" she said.[50]

The same student who borrowed $120,000 to attend Ohio Northern moved back in with her parents, and doesn't go out after work in order to save money. "When I was young I wanted to get out of Putnam County, get out of the cornfields," she told the *New York Times*. "I would love to get away. But it would be more financially responsible if I got a job near here and lived with my parents."[51]

Beyond merely delaying adulthood purchases and dampening the borrower's quality of life, several observers have even speculated that mounting amounts of student debt (and rising rates of default) pose a significant threat to the economy, much like the subprime mortgage market ultimately proved to be in 2007–08.

Data collected by the Department of Education, the largest student-loan lender in America, show that payments are being made on just 38 percent of the balance of federal student loans, down from 46 percent in 2007.[52] This reflects not only the desperate economic situation of many recent grads, but also the huge number of loans currently not in repayment because of in-school deferments (the standard practice when students are in school). The New York Federal Reserve Bank reported in March 2012 that one in four borrowers was delinquent on repayment, double the amount estimated.[53] William Brewer, the president of the National Association of Consumer Bankruptcy Attorneys, told *U.S. News and World Report*, "Take it from those of us on the frontline of economic distress in America: This could very well be the next debt bomb for the U.S. economy. . . . What we are worried about is that we are looking at the next mortgage-style debt threat to the United States."[54] Rajeev Date, the deputy director of the Consumer Financial Protection Bureau, echoes Brewer's concerns: "If one is not thinking about where this is headed over the next two or three years, you are just completely missing the warning signs."[55]

Just look at figure 1 produced by the New York Federal Reserve Bank. Compared to other forms of consumer debt (auto loans, mortgages, and credit card debt), delinquencies for student-loan debt have exploded in the last two years:

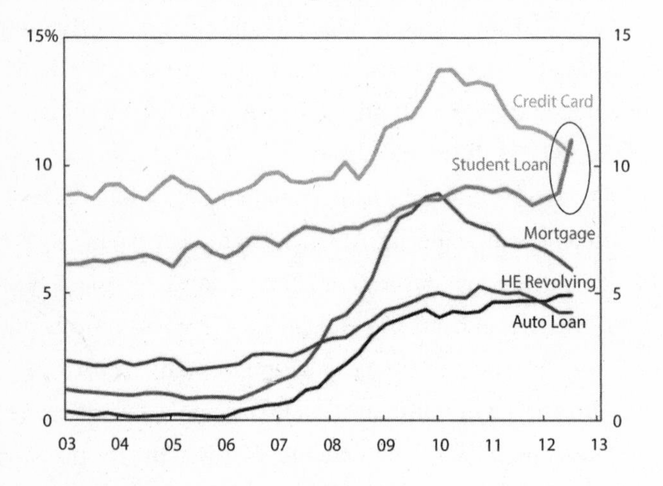

Figure 1. Percent of Balance 90+ Days Delinquent by Loan Type[56]

All told, runaway tuition fees weigh down the economy and threaten the livelihood of millions of American students. When private institutions decide to bill students more than $50,000 per year and costs at public institutions skyrocket, we must ask: Why are colleges charging so much in the first place? In the next chapter, we'll examine why college costs have spiraled out of control.

TWO

Creating a Financial Monster

Irresponsible borrowing is one of the main drivers of the higher education financial crisis, but it's not the only culprit. Some blame must fall on the colleges and universities themselves. They have done little, if anything, to control costs over the past several decades. The Bennett Hypothesis, as I (Bill) first articulated in the *New York Times* in 1987, states that the cost of college tuition will rise as long as the amount of money available in federal student-aid programs continues to increase with little or no accountability.[1]

I (Bennett) had noticed a telling phenomenon: Increases in federal financial aid were not improving college affordability as many policy makers and educators thought they would. While federal financial aid outlays increased, college tuitions continued to rise above and beyond the rate of inflation. Financial aid intended to make college more affordable for its recipients could rarely keep pace with increased tuition costs.

I (Bill) theorized that, much like the effects of subsidies on health care and the housing market, increasing student aid was insulating colleges from having to take market-driven cost-cutting measures, like improving productivity or efficiency. Colleges and universities knew full well that if they raised their tuition fees, financial aid outlays would likely increase in accordance, thereby ensuring that consumer demand—the great free market price regulator—did not suffer.

Twenty-five years later, the problem has worsened.

Federal lending policies continue to flood the higher education market with easy money. Record amounts of student aid are available to students, including those with little or no credit. Most problematic, an increasing amount of financial aid is going to middle-class students. Tuition costs have historically been held in check by the largest block of paying students, the middle class, and their earned incomes and expenses. Colleges cannot risk raising prices above what middle-class families can afford without fear of losing millions of students. But when middle-class students also receive easy loans, colleges have little holding them back from raising prices because upper-class students can afford increased tuition fees. In short, increasing loan availability raises price ceilings, rather than lowers them.

This problem went largely unnoticed until the recent economic recession. Job losses, home foreclosures, and earnings losses triggered mass defaults on student loans. The recession exposed a tremendous number of Americans who could no longer afford their loan debts and probably shouldn't have received loans in the first place.

Just as real estate agents and home builders benefited from the massive influx of easy money in the housing market in the early 2000s, so too do colleges and universities benefit from increases in financial aid. The more students take out loans and do not pay out of their own pockets, the less schools have to be wary of rising costs. For this reason, many schools are resistant to transparency or accountability. Very few students actually know the ultimate financial commitment they undertake when they attend college. If they did, they might not attend college at such a record rate.

Complicating matters, high tuition prices have become synonymous with prestigious and elite universities. Many parents are under the assumption that if tuition costs exceed $40,000 or $50,000 a year, their son or daughter must be getting a good education. At a few universities, like Harvey Mudd and Stanford, that can be the case. But at many others, the price only masks poor academics and training. In fact, many poorly performing universities have raised their prices to market themselves as elite, upper-class schools with the desired effect of attracting more applicants.

The higher education price model urgently needs reform. Other factors, like state education budgets and alumni donations, influence costs as well, but the biggest culprits are lenders (both private and the federal government) and college and university administrations.

What I wrote twenty-five years ago in the *New York Times* is still true today: "Higher education is not underfunded. It is under-accountable." Federal aid must be closely tied to academic performance, graduation rates, and the ability of students to repay their loans in a responsible manner if we are ever to rein in costs. This chapter explores how each of these players influences tuition costs and what must be done to control avalanching student indebtedness and make higher education more affordable.

Uncle Sam's Takeover

America's largest player in making student loans is the federal government. Uncle Sam's involvement with student loans has its origins in the National Defense Education Act (NDEA) of 1958. The bill was largely a response to the Soviet Union's launch of the *Sputnik* satellite in 1957, an event that told policy makers that America was lagging behind the Soviet Union in scientific and technical knowledge. Part of the NDEA stipulated that GIs and other individuals could obtain loans to attend college and acquire the skilled technology training that America needed to stay competitive with the Soviet Union.

Nineteen sixty-five was the watershed year for government involvement in the student-loan industry. Congress passed the Higher Education Act, which created Stafford Loans, the government's most popular loan program, which more than sixty million Americans have participated in to date to help pay for their education.[2] Stafford Loans guaranteed a low interest rate to the borrower as well as a six-month grace period before repayment at the time of graduating or withdrawing from school. Approximately 7.4 million students currently have subsidized Stafford Loans. The federal government holds about $902 billion of the nation's more than $1 trillion student-loan pool, most of which are Stafford Loans. According to the *New York Times*, the balance of federal student loans has actually grown by more than 60 percent in the past five years.[3]

The government's desire to stay involved in student lending was evident during the debate over Obamacare in 2010. In the run-up to the passage of the bill, Democrats added a provision (with the unfortunate acronym SLOP) known as the Student Loan Overhaul Proposal, which transferred control of the *federal* student-loan industry entirely to the Department of Education (although private banks and lending agencies may still make and service loans on their own). Previously, private lenders like Citigroup, Sallie Mae, and Nelnet had received guaranteed federal subsidies to lend money to students, with the government assuming nearly all the risk in case of borrower default. Now, students who wish to take on federal loans will deal entirely with the government.

Though it contained an estimated $61 billion in federal budget savings,[4] most of which was later negated by increased federal spending on Pell Grants (federal grants for the poorest students), there are several downsides to SLOP. Sarah Bauder, financial aid director at the University of Maryland, expressed her concern after the legislation was passed, theorizing, "The taxpayer will pay more in the long run because the Department of Education has to grow." Additionally, she said, "Direct lending, like health care reform, will take away competition, choice and innovation."[5]

When the government absorbs more functions from the private sector, the attendant administrative bloat increases, resulting in higher costs that are passed on to taxpayers. Richard Vedder, one of America's most influential and long-tenured scholars on higher education, echoed Bauder in pointing out the federal government's generally flawed student-loan policy by saying,

> In 2010 we moved to creating a monopoly in service provision. Any customer of the US Postal Service, the Bureau of Motor Vehicles, or liquor stores where there is a state monopoly knows that service is mediocre and inefficiently provided. The alternative model used prior to 2010 did use federal monies to finance the loans to students, and also federal interest rate subsidies, but allowed for different private firms to duke it out in the market for the right to "service" the loans. Companies provided loan counselors who described alternatives, and a student could talk to several of these. Today, I am told that there is a one-size-fits-all approach, one central website, and no individualized counseling. Most student financial aid administrators at colleges opposed the change to this system.[6]

Worst Practices

For all the control the federal government now assumes, one cannot trust it will assume a commensurate level of responsibility. In lending to students, the federal government violates or ignores simple, sound banking principles. Students with virtually no credit history are able to obtain fantastic sums of borrowed money for education, unlike requirements for business, mortgage, or auto loans. For example, borrowers at a higher risk of default (let's suppose these would include students with bad or little credit history or students majoring in subjects for which there is little demand) have the same interest rate as sound borrowers (students and families with good credit history or, hypothetically, engineering majors with a 3.7 grade point average). If a student defaults on his or her loan, taxpayers are denied the opportunity to recoup the money they have lent in the same manner that it would typically be paid back. In the worst-case scenarios, taxpayers wind up shouldering the bill for many unqualified borrowers. Nobody expects a student beginning college to have a sterling credit history, if he has one at all. But it is disconcerting that no mechanism is in place to evaluate borrowers' creditworthiness.

Stafford Loans are not all bad for the borrower, however. Most Stafford Loans have a fixed interest rate, meaning that borrowers are charged the same interest rate throughout the life of the loan and are not subject to variable rates that, depending on the baseline interest rate set by the Federal Reserve, have the potential to skyrocket and make repayment more expensive. Federal loans have borrowing limits, a form of consumer protection that allows the borrower to avoid high five- and six-figure loans. Other consumer protections that are guaranteed by federal loans but not private ones include income-based repayments, economic hardship deferments, and discharge in case of death or permanent disability. (See figure 2.)[7]

As shown by the chart below, federal loans are advantageous to the student, but not always to the taxpayer.

Figure 2. Paying Back Federal vs. Private Loans[8]

Options For Relief	Federal Loans	Private Loans
Extended Repayment	10 to 30 yrs	Some 15–30, Most 20–25
Graduated Repayment	Yes	No
Income-Contingent Repayment	Yes	No
Income-Sensitive Repayment	Yes	No
Income-Based Repayment	Yes	No
Loan Forgiveness Programs	Yes	No
In-School Deferment	Yes, unlimited	Yes, limited
Economic Hardship Deferment	Yes, 3 year cap	No
Forbearance	Yes, 3 year limit	Yes, 1 year limit
Closed School Discharge	Yes	No
Discharge In Student's Death	Yes	No (a few exceptions)
Discharge For Borrower's Permanent Disability	Yes	No
Bankruptcy Discharge	Yes (undue hardship)	Yes (undue hardship)

And yet, because Congress controls the fixed interest rates for Stafford Loans, they have become part and parcel of the federal government's irresponsible involvement in higher education. In July 2012 the interest rate on the subsidized Stafford Loans was set to double from 3.4 percent to 6.8 percent. Rather than engage in a meaningful debate over the effect of loan rates on college tuitions, Congress used the interest rate extension as a political weapon. Democrats, including the president, accused Republicans of wanting to raise tuition fees on students by allowing the loan rates to double. Congress eventually approved an extension of the existing Stafford Loan rates.

The backstory reveals just how recklessly Congress uses federal lending as a political cudgel at the expense of students. After taking back control of Congress in 2007, then Speaker Nancy Pelosi and the Democrats passed legislation that temporarily lowered the interest rates on the federally subsidized Stafford Loans from 6.8 percent to 3.4 percent. The extension would last until July 2012, when the rates would double to 6.8 percent, partly as a budget trick to offset the original costs.

The *Washington Post*'s editorial board called the whole ordeal "a campaign gimmick that Democrats cooked up to help them retake Congress in 2006. . . . It's expensive, it's poorly targeted, and it diverts attention and money from bigger problems facing federal support for higher education."[9] With the rates set to expire in the middle of election season, Democrats knew full well they could use the threat of rising interest rates against Republicans. They did exactly that. And Republicans cooperated by capitulating.

The problem with the loan rate extension is that it costs taxpayers $6 billion for this subsidy. And worse, it doesn't seem to be controlling costs. As we noted earlier, in 2011 alone, costs at the average public university rose more than 5 percent for in-state students, or about $1,100.[10] The average tuition at public universities rose more than 8 percent.[11] By comparison, the rate of inflation was 3 percent.[12] Democratic rhetoric over the federal student loan interest rate wrongly implies that an increase in the federal student loan interest rate would be utterly destructive to borrowers.[13] It wouldn't be. First, only about 9.5 million of the nation's 39 million outstanding student loans would be subject to a rate increase.[14] Secondly, if the current rate were to double, students would pay about $2,600 more over ten years. The effect of doubling the rates from 3.4 percent to 6.8 percent is minute when compared to the lifetime earnings of a person with a bachelor's degree (approximately $2.27 million).

By artificially lowering interest rates, the federal government keeps pumping easy loans to middle-class students, driving up tuition costs. The real problem here is the colleges and their unholy alliance with the federal government's loose purse strings subsidized by taxpayers.

The Bennett Hypothesis

Behind all the overwrought political platitudes—like "Let's make college more affordable"—is the assumption that more generous federal loans and grants will lower the cost of college for students. In actuality, easy access to federal student loans and grants has produced an increase in costs and, by extension, student indebtedness. As mentioned above, this is something I (Bill) first noticed more than twenty-five years ago during my tenure as US secretary of education (the Bennett Hypothesis: *College tuition will rise as long as the amount of money available in federal student aid programs continues to increase with little or no accountability*). Since then, federal loans have continued to increase and so have tuition prices.

In 2010, the Department of Education distributed $133 billion in student aid. In 2011, it was nearly $157 billion, an 18 percent increase. Pell Grants increased from $29 billion in 2010 to $36 billion in 2011, a 24 percent increase.[15] At the same time, in 2011, costs at the average public university rose 5.4 percent for in-state students, or about $1,100.[16] Average tuition at public universities rose 8.3 percent.[17] The increases have greatly outpaced the rate of inflation, which was 3 percent in 2011.[18]

Current US secretary of education Arne Duncan and others have countered that in years when federal aid has not increased, schools have still raised their prices. So perhaps a revised Bennett Hypothesis is in order: *Schools raise prices willy-nilly and subsidies follow, just to make it easier to swallow.*

While we acknowledge there is not a perfect correlation between financial aid and price increases on a year-to-year basis, the Bennett Hypothesis holds true in the aggregate. The College Board reports that since 1990, costs at public four-year colleges, the institutions enrolling a preponderance of today's students, have increased 150 percent. This despite the fact that over the same period, federal grants and tax benefits rose 242 percent. Federal loans have increased by a staggering 300 percent.[19] Similarly, others have said that reduced state funding for universities in recent years has pushed up costs much more than student aid. It is true that shrunken state budgets have hurt higher education (as we will examine later). But this alone doesn't account for a heightened trajectory of costs over the last thirty years. In fact, it supports our view. Between 1982 and 2007, college tuition and fees rose more than 400 percent (about four times the rate of inflation).[20] States have largely realized that as colleges capture student-loan dollars, thus turning themselves into increasingly self-funding entities, they can afford to be less dependent on state budget dollars. As a result of fewer subsidies from the states, schools raise prices. And the more they raise rates, the more they receive via student loans. It's a win-win for states and a lose-lose for taxpayers and students.

Last year, Andrew Gillen, a scholar at the Center for College Affordability and Productivity, authored a new paper introducing Bennett Hypothesis 2.0, an updated version of my original argument. Under the current financial aid system, he concluded that my old thesis was largely correct, writing, "As higher financial aid pushes costs higher, it inevitably puts upward pressure on tuition. Higher tuition, of course, reduces college affordability, leading to calls for more financial aid, setting the vicious cycle in motion all over again."[21]

Other researchers have also affirmed the validity of the Bennett Hypothesis. A study conducted by Claudia Goldin of Harvard University and Stephanie Riegg Cellini of George Washington University focused on 2,650 for-profit colleges and universities. They concluded that schools that received governmental support had tuition prices roughly 75 percent higher than those that do not.[22] In turn, they concluded that their observation lends . . . "credence to the 'Bennett hypothesis' that aid-eligible institutions raise tuition to maximize aid."[23] Mark Cuban, the technology billionaire, agrees. "You know who knows that the money is easy better than anyone?" he wrote in his blog post, "The Coming Meltdown in College Education," "The schools that are taking that student loan money in tuition. Which is exactly why they have no problems raising costs for tuition each and every year."[24]

Another acknowledgement of the Bennett Hypothesis came from Vice President Joe Biden. Follow this February 2012 exchange with a student at Florida State:

STUDENT: Good morning Mr. Vice President. I was wondering how do you feel about the idea that government subsidies and interference with the free market, for example, by artificially increasing availability of student loans is at least partially responsible for rising tuition costs. And now we're facing a possible student loan bubble and subsequent collapse just as we're coming out of the housing crisis.

BIDEN: Well, say the first part of your question again about how we're artificially creating what?

STUDENT: By manipulating variables in the free market and giving out government subsidies that maybe is partially responsible for rising tuition costs.

> **BIDEN**: By the way, government subsidies have impacted upon rising tuition costs. It's a conundrum here.[25]

It's actually not much of a conundrum. The problem is that politicians (quick to cater to the financial needs of young voters) and higher education institutions (addicted to federal loan dollars) have little interest in figuring it out.

As if to prove the point, a White House spokesman equivocated when attempting to clarify Biden's comments, saying, "There is no evidence to suggest that federal aid is a driver of tuition increases, but it's absolutely true that the formula we're using to distribute campus-based aid right now has not created the right incentives to bring down costs and promote affordability in higher education."[26] In short, forget the obvious answer, and posit some deeper mystery that allows politicians to avoid responsibility and continue pandering to voters at the expense of taxpayers.

More honest observers, however, continue to verify the Bennett Hypothesis. Peter Wood, president of the National Association of Scholars, recently confirmed the relationship between federal financial aid and tuition costs. Commenting on the higher education watchdog blog *Minding the Campus*, Wood described the sort of artificial tuition inflation he observed during his tenure at Boston University:

> Long before I knew it was called the "Bennett Hypothesis" I knew that colleges and universities increase tuition to capture increases in federal and state financial aid. I

> attended numerous meetings of university administrators where the topic of setting next year's tuition was discussed.
>
> *The regnant phrase was "Don't leave money sitting on the table."* The metaphoric table in question was the one on which the government had laid out a sumptuous banquet of increases of financial aid. Our job was to figure out how to consume as much of it as possible in tuition increases. This didn't necessarily mean we were insensitive to the needs of financially less well-off students. A substantial portion of the money we captured would be reallocated as "tuition discounts" or "institutional aid." *That is to say, just as Andrew Gillen observes, we combined Bennett Hypothesis-style capture of external student financial aid with "price discrimination."*[27]

Clearly, the Bennett Hypothesis has gained traction in many circles, including among university administrators.

Unintended Consequences

There is one exception to the Bennett Hypothesis: loans and grants for the neediest, low-income students. We should be giving federal aid to the students who need it the most—not middle- and upper-class students who have some means of paying for college. "[F]inancial aid . . . restricted to low income students," writes Gillen, "will therefore be more likely to succeed in making college more affordable and therefore accessible (for low income students). In contrast, universally available programs are more likely to simply fuel tuition increases and therefore more likely to fail to make college more affordable."[28] Giving federal subsidies to those who have more means of paying can accelerate tuition increases. As we've seen already, most middle- and upper-income students will go to college come hell or high water; their demand is highly insensitive to price. If colleges hike sticker prices, they will still come, and the loan programs merely add fuel to the tendency to hike fees.

But low-income students are extremely price sensitive. As tuition fees rise, applicants from low-income families fall off dramatically. So the college ends up with higher tuition fees and a higher proportion of rich kids who are getting a subsidy for a more expensive school. One study found that 20 percent of Pell grantees from families making more than $60,000 were attending schools that cost more than $30,000 per year.[29] There should be stricter means-tested standards for accepting Pell Grants so that those students who need them most can benefit, while those who don't do not drive up the cost for everyone.

Another unintended effect of giving Pell Grants and loans to middle- and high-income students has actually been to reduce the percentage of students attending college from low-income backgrounds. It is not a coincidence that the number of students from low-income backgrounds as a proportion of the college population has fallen over the last forty years as the mechanism of financial aid has grown. According to Richard Vedder, "In 1970, 12 percent of recent college graduates came from the bottom quartile of the income distribution; 40 years later, the percentage was 7.3 percent." In 1970 we didn't have Pell Grants, and the student loan program was in its infancy.[30] Subsidizing college costs has also been an increasing loss for taxpayers. For one, taxpayers are getting fewer returns for their money. In 2009, the six-year graduation rate of bachelor's students was 56 percent in the United States. In 1997, it was 52 percent. During that time period, student aid skyrocketed. According to the College Board, "total student aid increased by about 84% in inflation-adjusted dollars over the decade from 1997–98 to 2007–08," although the graduation rate ticked up only slightly.[31]

Regardless of whether students graduate or not, the federal government loans students money for college. When students fail to complete a degree or default on the loans, taxpayers have wasted their money on a failed investment. Clearly, taxpayers are subsidizing higher education at greater and greater costs while institutional performance has not kept up. This gap between enrollment and graduation costs the US economy millions of dollars in potential earnings each year and expands the growing student-loan bubble.

Distinguished professor and scholar Walter Russell Mead summarized the effect of federal lending policies this way: "The student loan system's biggest victims are exactly the people policy makers most want to help: marginal students whose chances of finishing are not great." He went on to explain why:

1. Federal support and available loans push up the costs of higher ed. Free money distorts the market in a big way.

2. Policy aimed at making college degrees more common increases the disadvantage for those who do not have or are unable to earn these degrees, and it adds to the pressure on everyone to at least give college a try.
3. When students fail at college, student loans become a permanent ball and chain for workers stuck at the low end of the labor market.[32]

What about For-Profits?

When it comes to institutional accountability for return on federal student loans, critics of higher education are often quick to attack for-profit higher education. If we examine some of the numbers surrounding for-profits (schools like the University of Phoenix, DeVry University, and Strayer University) and student borrowing, that criticism, at first glance, seems to be justified. For-profit students receive 25 percent of all federal student loans and grants, even though they make up only 11 percent of all college students.[33] In fact, one study conducted by the US Senate Health, Education, Labor, and Pensions Committee found that in 2009, 87 percent of the total revenues for fourteen for-profits came from the federal government. This means billions of dollars in loans and Pell Grants.[34] But despite the big dollars given to for-profit institutions, the results from public investment in for-profit students are underwhelming. Only 22 percent of all BA-seeking students at for-profit universities obtain their BA within six years, compared with 65 percent of students at nonprofit private schools and 55 percent of students at public institutions.[35] The US Senate Committee also found that 57 percent of enrollees at the same sixteen for-profit colleges studied ended up withdrawing from school within two years with no diploma.[36] And, in what is perhaps the most troubling statistic, the average indebtedness for the for-profit student is around $33,000, about $10,000 more than the average four-year graduate from a nonprofit institution.[37] This isn't surprising, however, when we consider that for-profits, on average, charge a higher tuition rate than nonprofit institutions.[38]

With these statistics in mind, it would be easy to label for-profits as abusers of federal student loan programs, or just flat-out greedy. But it's not that simple.

First, for-profits largely enroll students who come from challenging backgrounds. Seventy-six percent of students at for-profits do not file as dependents, a much higher percentage than students at nonprofits. This probably means that in addition to attending school, they are working to support themselves at the same time. Thirty-one percent of students at for-profits are single parents, and 51 percent of for-profit students have parents whose highest level of education attainment is a high school diploma. Forty-six percent of for-profit students are African American or Hispanic/Latino.[39] With a clientele that is often characterized by disadvantaged economic and educational backgrounds, it is, sadly, only inevitable that there will be a higher rate of attrition at for-profits than at nonprofits, where most of the students have the luxury of concentrating on school full-time, often relying on parents for financial support. Because so many students at for-profits are from low-income backgrounds, they must borrow more money than many traditional college students, and they have less time and money to devote to their educations. A single mother from a poor background who is trying to piece together a degree while working full-time is at a much higher risk for dropping out of school than a twenty-year-old from the suburbs. Far from being criticized for a poor-performing student body, for-profits deserve some commendation for accepting and enrolling students who would not otherwise have an opportunity to earn a college degree.

Second, in view of serving their disadvantaged population, for-profits offer nontraditional arrangements to their students that can be costly to the school: smaller classes; classes throughout the day, evening, and weekends; and larger career placement departments. And unlike nonprofit colleges and universities, for-profits are ineligible to receive tax exemptions, taxpayer subsidies, research and education grants, and state and local funding that can offset the cost of tuition. For-profit colleges and universities also pay taxes, which nonprofits are not required to do. All of this contributes to higher costs. In return, for-profits actually provide a significant amount of the skills training necessary to keep the American economy running, awarding 47 percent of all certificates and 21 percent of all associate's degrees.[40]

Still, for-profits are not flawless institutions. As profit-making enterprises, for-profits are very concerned with consistently enrolling new students. In furtherance of that goal, they often over promise the affordability and economic return of their product to often unsuspecting, uneducated individuals. Of course, this behavior is not characteristic of every or even most recruiters at for-profit colleges and universities, but it is happening. The *New York Times* examined the life of one woman who, by her own estimate, has tallied about $100,000 in debt from for-profit DeVry University. She dropped out after a few years and now makes $8.50 an hour. "I was promised the world and given a garbage dump to clean up," she said.[41] Another student who had briefly taken courses at the for-profit Collins College in Florida felt similarly ripped off after spending $12,000: "They were telling me everything I wanted to hear to get me in the door."[42] One whistleblower recalled in her testimony before the US Senate in 2010 the following experience pursuing prospective students while employed in the admissions department at the for-profit Argosy University, just one of many schools owned by EDMC (Education Management Corporation):

> We were constantly pressured to deliver a minimum of two applications per week. New "leads" were to be called three times a day for at least a week, then you could drop back to two, then one as the month progressed. Most of these leads were also being sold to the other online schools, so these poor people were inundated with phone calls mere minutes following their oftentimes unwittingly submitted information. These calls would continue to each of them for months.[43]

In response to the troubling data about for-profits and their graduates, Congress passed a new set of regulations on for-profits that seeks to rein in high student-loan default rates and correct the often low postgraduation employment among graduates of for-profits. A program must now be considered to lead to gainful employment if it meets at least one of the following three metrics: at least 35 percent of former students are repaying their loans (defined as reducing the loan balance by at least one dollar); the estimated annual loan payment of a typical graduate does not exceed 30 percent of his or her discretionary income; or the estimated annual loan payment of a typical graduate does not exceed 12 percent of his or her total earnings.

While ostensibly passed with good intentions, these new regulations raise an awkward question for their sponsors: why aren't nonprofit schools subject to the same restrictions? It strikes us that for-profits are being unfairly vilified for their students' poor prospects for repaying loans and getting hired in jobs for which they are trained. There is no question that there are tens of thousands, if not hundreds of thousands, of nonprofit, four-year graduates whose student loan payments exceed 35 percent of their discretionary income. And while 22.7 percent of all for-profit students default on their student loans, 18.3 percent of community college graduates do the same thing.[44] Why isn't the same standard of graduates' employment outcomes applied evenly to both for-profits and nonprofits alike?

Although sometimes accusations of for-profits abusing federal financial aid and over-recruiting students are justified, an appropriate response should not be to set unreasonable standards governing the entire industry. For one thing, nonprofits are beginning to offer more of the classes and learning options (especially online courses) that attract the students who typically enroll in for-profit education. Second, if policy makers are concerned about low-educated workers scrambling to enroll in expensive for-profit institutions to increase their competitiveness as workers, the best sort of reform to discourage this behavior is to (1) use K–12 education to build skills that employers covet and (2) increase opportunities for vocational education at the K–12 level. (We address both topics at length in the next chapter.) In the meantime, however, both for-profit and nonprofit institutions of higher education should be subject to the same standards of accountability on their receipt of federal aid and their employment of graduates.

Private Banks

On the other end of the lending spectrum are private banks. Like the federal government, banks spent much of the last two decades making loans to unqualified student borrowers. But unlike the federal government, they quickly learned the consequences of irresponsible lending. When the credit crunch of 2007 hit, banks realized that large amounts of loans with low interest rates, totaling somewhere in the neighborhood of $140 billion,[45] weren't as profitable as they had imagined. Additionally, as the credit crunch forced banks to realize they had fewer assets than originally thought, less capital became available to lend. And because of the subprime mortgage crisis, banks became scared of the consequences of lending money to students with no credit history and no real assets. They tightened up liberal lending practices as a result.

Since then, banks have been divided in their willingness to make loans. Some, like Royal Bank of Scotland (RBS) and Wells Fargo, are increasing their position—largely because students need to borrow more than what the federal limits will allow a student to borrow. Timothy Sloan, the CFO of Wells Fargo, told the *Wall Street Journal*, "The last time I checked, a third of the people in this country go to college and a good portion of those need to borrow some money to do that."[46] Certain banks are now offering loans with interest rates as low as 5.75 percent for borrowers with good credit—a full point lower than the 6.8 percent for many federal loans.[47]

At RBS, 90 percent of loans are cosigned.[48] This represents a responsible step forward in student-lending habits that more banks would be wise to adopt.

But some banks, like J. P. Morgan, U.S. Bancorp, and Citigroup, are minimizing their involvement in student loans or getting out entirely.

Although borrowing from a private bank has advantages in its absence of borrowing limits and (speaking from experience) an easier borrowing process, there are still downsides to borrowing from private lenders. Some private lenders, unlike the government, have a history of attaching extremely high interest rates to their loans and, as in the subprime mortgage mess, have not always been transparent in disclosing to borrowers the final costs of the loan, once interest is calculated. One student in 2000 took a loan from Wells Fargo to attend school. He claims his loan documents said he would pay off his loan by 2010. Instead, after six years of steady repayments he still owed one hundred dollars more on his loan than when he started.[49] Another private lender outright lied to borrowers about what they could use their student loans for and when they could be obtained.[50] It's no surprise that the rates of student default are higher on private student loans than federally backed ones, where smaller borrowing amounts and lower interest rates make repayment easier. But in general, most private lenders have operated honestly.

A recurrent theme in complaints about private loans focuses on the borrower's unawareness of the final cost of a loan and in particular how much the cost would ultimately be. This indicates the malpractice of private lenders *and* the ignorance of borrowers. One young woman who graduated from Tufts University in Boston borrowed $49,000 to pay for school. "How bad could it be?" she remembers thinking. But on graduation day, she was looking at a total of $65,000 once interest rates were calculated, some at 13 percent.[51]

Borrowers need to be vigilant to understand how much debt they are taking on once interest is calculated, and that declaring bankruptcy is not an option with private loans. Carefully examine every contract before you sign it. Get your parents, and if possible, some other knowledgeable party to review it too. The terms of private loans frequently offer less flexibility than federal loans in the amount that must be paid back each month, the time frame when repayment must occur, and the ability to obtain a deferment for a loan.[52]

We saw this toxic borrower unawareness reflected in the Occupy Wall Street movement, the most prominent, popular expression of anger over student loans. Many of the protesters felt ripped off by big banks. But, broadly speaking, their consternation is misplaced. Their anger is directed at private banks, that, at risk to themselves, made large loans to students with no credit history, so that they may obtain a college education. These banks require little to no proof of academic potential or repayment ability. A good credit score or cosigner will help students get the needed money at a cheaper rate, but few loans are outright denied. Would the protesters rather the banks not make the loans at all, jeopardizing their ability to pay for a coveted college education?

While student debt is a centerpiece of the Occupy Wall Street movement, the real issue is one of unfulfilled expectation. Simply, many Occupiers concerned with student debt are not seeing the return on investment that they once anticipated, and it makes them angry. "I have $50,000 in student loan debt and my B.A. is useless," said one of those associated with the movement.[53] And another stated, "I was led to believe that college would insure me a job. I now have $40,000 worth of student debt."[54]

As Mark Cuban said, the impression of most borrowers was that they would "flip" a very expensive education for a well-paying job. For many Occupiers, this did not happen, and the angst over student debt is so great that they will resort to civic indecency, like assaulting police officers or defacing public property. Their actions are inexcusable, but with a miserable job market for recent graduates, their agitation is understandable, although misguided.

It's important to remember, however, that not everyone with debt wants a bailout. Christina Hagan, a twenty-three-year-old who valued a Christian education and graduated with more than $65,000 in student debt, takes a great deal of personal responsibility for her situation: "I placed a priority on a Christian education and I didn't think about the debt. I need my generation to understand that nothing is free."[55]

One Occupier, posting in an online forum, shared a similar sentiment. "Nobody has ever held a gun to my head and said 'here sign this student loan' nobody has ever told me I would ever be rich once I get my degree. We are responsible for our own actions and the decisions we make," he wrote.[56] But many, even if they acknowledge their own responsibility for their circumstances, are still left feeling suckered into purchasing an education with seemingly little value.

The Scarcity Scam

Value hinges on price, and the price model of higher education is terribly skewed, even before one takes into account loans and tuition costs. In the current model of college pricing, colleges compete on the basis of prestige, not price. They frequently raise their costs to give the impression that their product is of higher value than the next school's—an academic "arms race," as our friend Richard Vedder has described it.[57]

Students fall prey to this scam because they too easily equate a high price with high quality. What's more, they too easily assume a positive correlation between the cost of their degrees and their opportunities in the job market, leading them to shoulder higher levels of debt. But the psychology gets trickier still. Since student loans are counted under "financial aid," students think they're getting a bargain when they look at the reduced sticker price—never mind that they still have to pay the full amount. Schools then capture the student's tuition dollars in the form of his student loan, regardless of whether the student learns anything along the way, graduates, or obtains a job after graduation. Explains Arizona State University president Michael Crow, a genuine reformer in the world of higher education:

> Unlike other sectors, higher education is dominated by a model in which status is attained through the maintenance of scarcity. Such scarcity is sanctioned by tradition and attainted through exclusivity. Historically, status hasn't been measured through impacts on local, state, or national socioeconomic success, nor achieved through indicators of innovation or reductions to the cost of learning.[58]

In lieu of real indicators of a college's worth, students and parents are left with the proxy indicator of price. Since the schools can control that, it's like they get to grade their own papers, so to speak. Generally, the higher a school costs, the more people are apt to believe it provides a quality education.

In the early 1990s, just as the cost of college was starting to explode, the Department of Justice accused several Ivy League universities of price-fixing. They had all agreed that each school would award as much financial aid as possible to applicants admitted to more than one of the Ivies, so that the applicants wouldn't actually have to base attendance at one of the schools on the cost.

"The defendants conspired to eliminate cost competition as a factor in choosing a college," Attorney General Dick Thornburgh confirmed. "The choice of whether to consider price when picking a school belongs to parents and students, not the college or university."[59]

Essentially, the Ivies couldn't handle the idea that a student would choose a non-Ivy college of lower cost, even if the allure of the Ivy name were missing. If hundreds of top-tier candidates did so, it might diminish the prestige of Cornell or Columbia, and check-cutting parents would start to think twice about how much an Ivy League degree was really worth, and—*gasp!*—even start sending their kids to Georgetown or Tufts. As was true then, colleges today are falsely portraying high tuition prices as a metric of value.

Perhaps the most visible evidence of the prestige illusion is the *U.S. News and World Report* college rankings. The famed rankings are tremendously popular. When *U.S. News* published the rankings in 2011, its Web traffic spiked to ten million hits that month, considerably higher than the norm.[60] Colleges know the significance of these rankings. To get a glimpse of the obsession, take the case of George Washington University (GWU). Knowing how important the rankings are to parents and students thinking about college, GWU submitted misleading statistics about its students' academic performance to *U.S. News* in hopes of ascending the rankings ladder. *U.S. News* found out and booted GWU from the rankings entirely. These rankings are (mistakenly) considered the gold standard for determining which schools are good and which are not.

But the rankings are problematic at best. Six researchers weigh an arbitrary number of variables to produce a list of one hundred schools deemed the "Best Colleges." The highest-weighted variable is "undergraduate academic reputation," accounting for 22.5 out of 100 possible points. "Faculty resources" is 20 points, and "student selectivity" is 15 points. "Alumni giving" is 5 points. These factors are not entirely worthless in considering the value of a school, but it is hard for the average college consumer to understand how these criteria reflect upon the desirability of a school. Moreover, what would seem like crucial criteria—for example, employability upon graduation and affordability—are not given at all. "Graduation rate performance" is given only 7.5 points.

Further complicating matters, these rankings compare entirely different schools. As Malcolm Gladwell wrote in his excellent essay on the subject, Penn State, a massive state institution, is judged to be 1 point better than Yeshiva University, a small, private Jewish school in Manhattan. How can these two entirely different institutions be reasonably compared to each other? They can't, says Gladwell. "Sound judgments of educational quality have to be based on specific, hard-to-observe features. But reputational ratings are simply inferences from broad, readily observable features of an institution's identity, such as its history, its prominence in the media, or the elegance of its architecture. They are prejudices."[61]

Every year, new students fall prey to the fancy vagaries of college rankings and appealing brochures. Cheesy catch phrases like "follow your dreams" and "success is only a degree away" tantalize incoming students who don't know any better. The University of Dayton's promotional materials described its product as "a lifetime investment, appreciating over the course of time."[62] In reality, college should come with a bright red warning label: "Warning! High risk of debt and unemployment." Universities will do anything to avoid these warnings. "[A]void bad words like 'cost,' 'pay,' . . . 'contract' and 'buy' in your piece and avoid the conflicting feelings they generate," advised a 2009 cover article in *Enrollment Management* on the topic of writing admissions copy. "There are direct marketing 'words' that can make or break your piece," added the article.[63]

With a ubiquitous guarantee for federal subsidies for education in place, most schools know that they can rope impressionable students into signing on the dotted line, without giving them the full story. "Aid administrators want to keep their jobs," said Joan H. Crissman, chief executive of the National Association of Student Financial Aid Administrators. "If the administration finds out that you're encouraging students to go to a cheaper school just because you don't think they can handle the debt load, I don't think it's going to mesh very well."[64] One young woman who attended Anderson University in Ohio described the school's approach as, "It's doable and normal to go into that much debt."[65]

In fairness, we do not mean to suggest that every administrator at every school is looking to suck up as many federal dollars as possible. After all, tuition is the lifeblood of higher education.

Many schools offer some form of financial literacy tutorial or noncredit course, such as the Bevonomics course at the University of Texas at Austin.[66] But more are needed. It's time for education consumers to make decisions with their wallets, not just their hearts.

In 2012, a consortium of colleges representing 1.4 million students, including Arizona State and the state university systems of New York, Maryland, Texas, and Massachusetts, came together to agree on a new standardized financial aid form that clearly states the cost of a year of classes, the student's net cost after grants and scholarships, financial aid options to pay that cost, and estimated monthly payments for federal loans. Secretary of education Arne Duncan described the move as "basic transparency."[67] We praise the schools involved for their efforts, but the fact that only now are schools agreeing to something like a standardized disclosure document (as is common in the mortgage industry) evidences the fact that colleges have prioritized capturing students' and federal money over their students' long-term financial interest.

Skin in the Game and Other Solutions

The best medicine to reform universities pushing easy money on their students would be to increase their financial stake in their students' outcomes. They need to have more skin in the game.

What I (Bill) said twenty-five years ago holds true today. Higher education is not underfunded. It is under-accountable. Schools, despite capturing huge sums of money in the form of students' loans, parents' paychecks, and donors' wallets, have very little accountability for their students' performances. As we have seen, colleges dole out vast sums of federal aid in the form of Pell Grants and loans (the most common being the Stafford Loan), but they suffer no consequences if their students don't graduate, if they are saddled with unbearable amounts of debt, or if their loans default.

Even President Barack Obama has agreed that colleges need to be held more accountable when they push tuition higher. "We are putting colleges on notice," he said in a speech to students at the University of Michigan in 2012. "[Y]ou can't assume that you'll just jack up tuition every single year. If you can't stop tuition from going up, then the funding you get from taxpayers each year will go down. We should push colleges to do better. We should hold them accountable if they don't."[68]

One sensible solution would be to tie more lending to *academic persistence*, that is, a borrower's proven ability to succeed in the classroom. Currently, a mediocre student at a mediocre school is eligible for the same federally backed loan as an MIT student studying math. Let's recalibrate student lending to favor those students who are at a lower risk for default. Not every single loan should be considered on the basis of academic performance or economic utility, but this is a meritocratic approach that also favors taxpayers and is consistent with how mortgages and other loans are formulated.

Another possibility would be for each college to pay a fee for every one of its students who defaults on a student loan, or have a 10 to 20 percent equity stake in each loan that originates at its school. By increasing each college's stake in its students' borrowing choices, we are confident that more schools would impose stricter standards on who could obtain student loans. Alex Pollock, formerly a mortgage banker and now a scholar at the American Enterprise Institute, developed a mortgage portfolio in the 1990s that spread credit risk to the mortgage originators themselves, a practice that was not employed by many lending institutions. The result was a portfolio that accumulated only half the losses that government-backed mortgage giants Fannie Mae and Freddie Mac did, even before the financial crisis.[69] By not transferring the risk to someone else, these lenders made prudent decisions that benefited them and their borrowers in the long run.

Another practical suggestion would be to limit student loans for living expenses, or impose means testing for how much of a loan could go for living expenses. The Department of Education estimates that living at home during college can save roughly $6,000 per year.[70] Many students borrow large sums of money to live a more lavish lifestyle than previous generations of college students. "I've seen it over and over again," said Anne Walker, director of student financial services at Rice University. "If you live like a professional while a student, you'll live like a student while a professional."[71]

There's also the possibility of cutting out the middleman.

Colleges capture federal student-loan money directly to use for whatever purposes they wish. What if we established private equity relationships between students and investors?[72] University of Chicago professor Luigi Zingales proposed just this in his 2012 *New York Times* article, "The College Graduate as Collateral." Students and investors would come together in private exchanges designed to match students with investors. In return for financing part of a student's college education, an investor would receive a portion of the student's future income.

This again is a meritocratic system that would reduce the administrative bloat in the federal government and college financial aid offices, as well as cut out risk to taxpayers. And it incentivizes students to work harder. Investors would be more likely to invest in students who had majors that resulted in higher rates of unemployment—obviating the supply for the mediocre sociology major. As Zingales puts it, "The most important effect of these equity contracts would be to show that it is possible to intervene to help the disadvantaged without turning that help into an undue subsidy for the producers (universities) and the creation of a privileged class (professors like me) at the expense of everybody else (students and taxpayers)."[73]

Other Factors Subsidizing Prestige

We have discussed at length the abundance of federal money as one of the biggest factors pushing up college costs. But other factors have sent costs soaring in recent years. Peter Wood, the former Boston University administrator whom we quoted earlier, also talked to *Minding the Campus* about why colleges were so greedy to capture federal dollars each year:

> [W]e did all this in the pursuit of educational excellence. It was a large private university in the shadow of world-ranked neighbors and it was attempting to pull itself up in the world of prestige and influence by its bootstraps. There were townhouses that needed buying; laboratories that needed building; faculty stars that needed hiring; classrooms and residence halls that needed refurbishing; symphonies that needed performing; grotesque modern sculptures that needed displaying; and administrators that needed chauffeuring.[74]

Set foot on virtually any college campus, and you can see the evidence that colleges are competing on the idea of prestige, not price, and are in large part using student loan dollars to do it. Colleges want to give the impression to students and parents that they will provide a superior quality of learning, comfort, and recreation over other colleges. But these are often frivolous and expensive pursuits, unessential to the mission of educating students. Let's take a closer look at some of the ways that colleges are misusing tuition dollars.

High-Paid Faculty?

Schools, especially state-run institutions, often cry poor mouth over budget cuts but are spending millions on faculty who earn generous salaries, even though they contribute little to student achievement, original research, or both. Many times, they earn stunning benefits, accrued over the course of a lifetime, which few other professions enjoy.

David Rubenstein, a recently retired University of Illinois professor, published this account in a piece in the *Weekly Standard* in 2011:

> After 34 years of teaching sociology at the University of Illinois at Chicago, I recently retired at age 64 at 80 percent of my pay for life. This calculation was based on a salary spiked by summer teaching, and since I no longer pay into the retirement fund, I now receive significantly more than when I "worked." But that's not all: There's a generous health insurance plan, a guaranteed 3 percent annual cost of living increase, and a few other perquisites. Having overinvested in my retirement annuity, I received a fat refund and—when it rains, it pours—another for unused sick leave. I was also offered the opportunity to teach as an emeritus for three years, receiving $8,000 per course, double the pay for adjuncts, which works out to over $200 an hour. Another going-away present was summer pay, one ninth of my salary, with no teaching obligation. . . .
>
> Why do I put "worked" in quotation marks? Because my main task as a university professor was self-cultivation: reading and writing about topics that interested me.[75]

Rubenstein's experience is not the norm for college professors everywhere—indeed, most young professors are barely subsisting on low-wage adjunct jobs—but it highlights one aspect of the professoriate that is underreported: excessive salaries and benefits. According to the Bureau of Labor Statistics, the average salary for a full professor is almost $109,000 per year.[76] There's nothing inherently wrong with paying someone well, but schools (especially state schools) have little right to complain about cuts when many professors are earning high salaries and enjoying cushy working arrangements like setting their own schedules, teaching in class approximately nine to twelve hours a week for thirty weeks a year, delegating work to graduate students, and taking advantage of often-free on-campus amenities like exercise facilities.

Granted, there is an outside-the-classroom component of teaching that involves lesson planning, department meetings, and so on. But as in Rubenstein's case, many professors are earning lavish salaries for less work than students, parents, and taxpayers deserve for their money.

One case study by Richard Vedder and the Center for College Affordability and Productivity found the following at the University of Texas at Austin:

> 20 percent of UT Austin faculty are teaching 57 percent of student credit hours. They also generate 18 percent of the campus's research funding. This suggests that these faculty are not jeopardizing their status as researchers by assuming such a high level of teaching responsibility. Conversely, the least productive 20 percent of faculty teach only 2 percent of all student credit hours and

> generate a disproportionately smaller percentage of external research funding than do other faculty segments.[77]

This indicates that many professors are not earning their salaries by either research or teaching. This study shows that teaching does not have to be sacrificed for research or vice versa. The bottom line, says Vedder, is that, "Simply by having faculty teach more students or courses, students and taxpayers will benefit significantly by reduced university costs."[78]

We suspect that the situation of underworked professors is similar at many other schools. We, too, would like to see costs for students go down by having professors' workloads go up, thus obviating the need for further hiring of similarly underworked professors or overworked, underpaid adjuncts.

Administration Costs

The costs of administration (and especially high-paid administrators) are also driving up costs for colleges that are passed on in tuition hikes. There seems to be no better example than the former president of American University (AU) in Washington, DC, Ben Ladner. After becoming president in 1994 at a salary of $225,000, Ladner received a series of pay increases that culminated in his receiving more than $880,000 a year by 2004, making him one of the highest-paid college presidents in the country.

But that was only the beginning. Ladner also received an expense account from the university, and he made liberal use of it. AU purchased a residence for Ladner and renovated it to his liking, spending $200,000 in the process, including

$30,000 for a waterfall and pond behind the patio. His contract stipulated AU would pay for "housekeeping services and residence staff" at his home, as well as "full use" of a car and driver, not only for him but also for his wife.

Ladner ordered a collection of medals made for himself—eight in total—to wear at AU's graduation ceremonies. But eventually, he began expensing items to the university that had no bearing on his official business—an engagement party, a French chef, one-hundred-dollar bottles of wine. In the end, the university's sanction of a lavish lifestyle proved a moral hazard, and the board terminated Ladner for misappropriation of funds.[79]

Now, in fairness, American University's reputation greatly increased during Ladner's tenure. It attracted more competitive students, and its schools of international service and law are considered very strong. The AU of 2005 was certainly not the AU of 1994. And there is something to be said for paying skilled money-raisers an appropriate salary to retain them. But a college president is perfectly capable of conducting his duties without a $45,000 per-year personal assistant—*for his wife.*[80]

We hold nothing against profit-generating universities and how they choose to allocate their resources. However, if the true interest of higher education is the best interest of students, students should know what their valuable tuition dollars are financing. We are arguing not for salary caps or price controls but for transparency and accountability. Students put great trust and resources into colleges and universities; the least they can get in return is an honest bill of sale. Higher education would be far better off if students were treated like stockholders and not merely consumers.

Unfortunately, the type of compensation that Ladner enjoyed is not unusual. Though the bulk of Ohio State president E. Gordon Gee's salary is paid for by a university foundation and not taxpayers, he is still given a generous expense account, and one of those expenses is the use of a private jet. According to an analysis of information provided by Ohio State to the *Dayton Daily News*, "Ohio State pays $22,500 per month for an ownership share in NetJets and a fixed rental rate of $7,941 per month, plus $1,950 per flight hour. The university contracts for 150 flight hours per year, with up to 100 of those hours earmarked for Gee's use."[81] The amount paid by Ohio State for Gee's plane over one year is more than the governor of Ohio has paid in the past five years for private jet flights. Hold that in mind while considering Gee's thoughts on today's cost of college. "I readily admit it," he told the *New York Times*, "I didn't think about costs. I do not think we have given significant thought to the impact of college costs on families."[82] We agree.

Perhaps the worst cases of excessive compensation paid to top administrators have been occurring for years in California. Arguably the most financially imperiled state in the country, California has seen budget cuts take a toll on its higher education system. The University of California (UC) and Cal State (CSU) systems have each been cut by more than $1 billion over the last two years, and each faced an additional $200 million in cuts in the fall of 2012. What's more, California community colleges have experienced more than

$800 million in cuts in the last three years.[83] Students are being denied admission, and tuition is rising as a result.

Yet, the leadership of both the Cal State and the UC systems have been selfish and recalcitrant in their refusal to take on personal sacrifices to help preserve their systems as much as possible. In July 2011, the Cal State Board of Trustees voted to raise student tuition by 12 percent. "Literally moments later," reported *Inside Higher Ed*, the same board voted a $100,000 pay increase for the president of San Diego State University, bringing his pay to $400,000—$350,000 of which came from state funds.[84]

But the CSU trustees weren't finished. The *San Diego Tribune* reported that in March 2012, "CSU trustees approved 10 percent pay hikes for two campus presidents just as administrators outlined a plan for sweeping cuts that will deny admission to thousands of students."[85] The plan in question allowed for base salaries in excess of over $300,000 for each of the two presidents, as well as a $12,000 car allowance for each and a $60,000 housing expense for one of them. Eventually, CSU agreed to freeze taxpayer-funded levels of compensation but still allowed for pay increases paid for by nonprofit campus foundations, where money is often used to pay for things like student scholarships, academic programs, or student services. The amounts of compensation in question will not solve the Cal State system's budget woes, but they reflect the fact that some highly paid administrators and board members may be more concerned with their own wants than they are with the needs of students.

One situation with the highest-ranking University of

California executives is even more embarrassing. California is in the midst of an enormous public-sector pension crisis, having committed more money and benefits to public-sector employees statewide than it can afford to pay. The UC system alone, having failed to contribute to the pension fund over the course of twenty years, owes at least $6.3 billion to its current and future retirees. In light of such dire circumstances, it is astonishing that in December 2010, thirty-six highly paid executives of the UC system, representing two hundred highly paid UC executive employees in total, sent a letter to the UC's Board of Regents protesting potential pension cuts. At the time, the board was reconsidering an agreement forged in 1999 that stipulated pensioners in the UC system could be compensated with amounts relative to their full salaries, not a $245,000 cap previously set by the IRS. With pension reform under way in California, the executives sensed their fat-cat pensions would be cut. They insisted that the UC Regents had "legal, moral and ethical obligation" to adhere to the 1999 agreement, even though these executives' pensions alone would cost taxpayers $61 million.[86]

Every year the regents must approve the agreement, and the clamor indicates once again that some highly paid administrators (who are also public employees) think of their entrenched interests above those of students and taxpayers. Chris Edley, one of the leaders of the effort and the dean of UC Berkeley School of Law, who earns $350,000 per year, defended the move by saying, "I accept the criticism of me personally for insisting that UC stick to a promise that is financially important to my family."[87] This comment smacks of a statement that former NBA star Latrell Sprewell made in 2004, when he said a three-year $21-million contract wasn't enough money because "I've got my family to feed."[88] Thankfully, the UC Regents rejected the pension increases in 2012.

The situation in the University of California system reflects a larger truth about the skyrocketing cost of college: there is an ever-growing amount of administrative bloat that must be sustained by student dollars. According to Jay Greene, a professor at the University of Arkansas, "Between 1993 and 2007, the number of full-time administrators per 100 students at America's leading universities grew by 39 percent, while the number of employees engaged in teaching, research or service only grew by 18 percent. Additionally, inflation-adjusted spending on administration per student increased by 61 percent."[89] Although there has been a significant increase in the number of students attending college in that time period, as of 2007, "it took 13.1 percent more employees to educate the same number of students than it did in 1993."[90]

Why is this? First, a school needs to hire additional administrators to manage numerous programs that are not a part of their essential mission of educating students—things like managing federal aid, administering athletic programs (a costly drain for many schools), and establishing offices for supervising a school's diversity in race, gender, and sexual orientation. Andrew Hacker and Claudia Dreifus, in their book *Higher Education?*, counted seventy-three fund-raising staffers, a twenty-nine-person art museum staff, a "babysitting coordinator," a "spouse/partner employment coordinator," and a "queer life coordinator" at tiny Williams College, my (Bill's) alma mater.[91] Jay Greene speculates that schools are growing their administrations precisely because they *can*. As schools capture huge amounts of federal dollars in the forms of student loans, they can afford to be more profligate, and enlarge different offices or departments depending on the whims of intracampus politics or largesse.

Novel and Redundant Academic Programs

Another avoidable drain on university budgets is the proliferation of academic programs that are expensive to maintain but do little to demonstrate their worth to students. We do not mean to indict time-tested disciplines like Greek and Latin, music, or mathematics that may be under fire because of budget constraints and lack of student interest. Rather, we are referring to academic programs such as the Popular Culture Studies program (Ohio State), the graduate program (PhD only) in History of Consciousness (University of California at Santa Cruz), and lesbian, gay, bisexual, transgender, and queer studies (nearly everywhere), which have questionable academic value and do little to prepare students for the workplace. (We'll address the purely academic dimensions of such programs in a later chapter.) But the attendant costs of the faculty and administration of such programs, and the fact that they produce graduates who have few job skills for the workplace, lead us to question how necessary they really are.

In this regard, American universities might take a look at

what China is doing. In 2011, the *Wall Street Journal* reported that China, seeing many graduates unable to find jobs, planned to cancel college majors in which the employment rate for graduates falls below 60 percent for two consecutive years.[92] This heavy-handed solution should not be a policy entertained by the US government (indeed, one of the first majors to go would be US history if that were the case). But colleges should think hard about eliminating trendy majors that consistently do not demonstrate their intellectual rigor, fiduciary worth, or ability to produce employable graduates. The same can be said for graduate programs.

State university systems should also consider cutting duplicative academic programs, majors with limited enrollment that are offered across multiple campuses. Ohio governor John Kasich, who has faced difficult budget cuts to higher education in his state, has described the problem as "not just inefficiencies. . . . It's, 'I want to be the best in this.' It's duplication of resources. It's a sweeping change that is needed across academia."[93] Kasich has a point. Why should multiple campuses in the same state-funded university system offer the same low-demand, high-unemployment major, such as journalism or sociology? When every school strives to have every program, it produces a glut of qualified graduates and functions as a duplicative waste of resources.

Expensive and Unnecessary Amenities and Student Programs

At the same time, colleges and universities are beginning to look less like places of higher learning and more like luxury resorts. Boston University's new $200-million fitness facility features a thirty-five-foot rock-climbing wall. At Davidson College in North Carolina, the college will wash, dry, and fold laundry for its students.[94]

In 2012, *Businessweek* magazine profiled High Point University, a small college in North Carolina. High Point is no different from any other college competing on reputation to gain customers (students). The writer of the piece noticed a number of amenities entirely unknown to students a generation ago, including a mechanized mini-train that runs through campus, marble floors in the business center, a first-rate movie theater, a steakhouse, dorms with plasma-screen TVs, and an outdoor hot tub at the $19-million Greek life facility. President Nido Qubein, a former motivational speaker, says his plan is "to create an environment in which [students] aspire to become extraordinary." To do that, High Point must stand out. "High Point can no longer swim in an ocean of sameness," he said.[95]

So far that's meant $700 million in improvements, and High Point is swimming in an ocean of debt, not sameness: $77 million of it. But a clean, new look can make a college more attractive to wealthy students paying more attention to the school's aesthetics than its quality of learning. The college captures their fees to pay for improvements, and the college doesn't feel as bad raising tuition, since wealthier students can absorb an increase more easily (and everyone else can get a student loan). One piece in *Sky*, the Delta Air Lines in-flight magazine, fawned over High Point's expansion, without asking where all the money for the project was coming from, or questioning what returns such investments provide.[96]

To attract those students who can afford more out of pocket, Qubein has almost doubled admissions staff, run a $500,000 print and TV ad campaign in North Carolina, and sent admissions officers to hundreds of high schools in the northeastern and mid-Atlantic states, often the locus of elite and moneyed private schools. "The world is marveling at how High Point University has grown so successfully in the midst of the worst economic times in 54 years,"[97] said Qubein.

But Qubein is merely applying a sheen of glass, bricks, and hot tubs to an academically lukewarm institution. High Point charges close to $43,000 per year in tuition, room, board, and fees, but its average student SAT score is a combined 1,100 for reading and math, only about 100 points better than the average score. Only 69 percent of its faculty have a terminal degree, an acceptable but not impressive number.

And yet students still come to High Point, largely on the strength of its aesthetic appeal. One student from Rhode Island (appropriately interviewed in the hot tub) said, "With all the amenities, the school can't be beat." A donor said Qubein told him in 2005, "This university needs a face-lift, or we're not going to be able to get the right kind of client."[98] High Point is creating the impression that a beautiful campus is an academically strong one. The emperor should be feeling the breeze. The writer of the piece describes Qubein's pitch to prospective parents:

> Moving to the edge of the stage, he picks up a bag of Hershey's Kisses and a box of Godiva chocolates. The Hershey candy cost about $4, he informs the audience; the Godiva, $40. "Both are good," he says, "but only one resides in the extraordinary. It presents itself in a way that people find compellingly good." He leans toward the audience, the Godiva box in the palm of his right hand. "Isn't that what you want for your child?"[99]

Students and parents are easily allured by the bells and whistles of new facilities. But these amenities are not cheap, and they suck up valuable student dollars. Moreover, their gleam obscures the ability of students and parents to evaluate a college on the basis of the most important factor: academic quality. There is no premium for a dorm room with HBO than one without it. With the percentage of students with student loans growing, why should students continue to subject themselves and taxpayers to this misuse of resources?

The States

Twenty-nine states allocated less money to higher education in 2011–12 than they did in 2006–07.[100]

The main reason is that states have had to pay for higher public health care costs (often with shrinking tax bases) and thus have had to take money from higher education. But another reason for decreased funding over recent years has been that lawmakers have figured out schools could support themselves as moneymaking entities by charging higher prices and capturing more loan dollars. We do not mean to suggest that all colleges have been eager merely to rip off students. There is a role for state governments in supporting higher education, and it brings us no pleasure to see states taking an axe to higher education budgets. But especially in light of reduced public funds for higher education, public institutions should be making every effort to steward their resources in a way that honors their students and taxpayers.

THREE

So Is It Worth It?

In fifty years . . . you're going to come up with the fact that . . . you dropped one hundred and fifty grand on [an] . . . education that you could have got for a dollar fifty in late charges at the public library!" So says Will Hunting to a Harvard student in *Good Will Hunting*.[1] Though the movie was released in 1997, Hunting's line presaged the most important debate concerning higher education today: Is college worth the high cost? Does it provide a degree of economic security and personal happiness that cannot be found elsewhere? Taking into account the high risk of debt and unemployment or underemployment, does the end justify the means? Should everyone go to college?

Apparently, many Americans think so. In 1960, fewer than 10 percent of Americans twenty-five years and older had a college degree. By 2012, the number was a little more than 30 percent, even while college has become—as we've seen—increasingly more expensive.

As we pointed out in chapter 1, college enrollment today

has even been described by some as the default activity for graduating high school seniors. With 33 percent of all Americans ages twenty-five to twenty-nine in possession of a BA, that suggestion doesn't look far off.[2]

So Why Do We Go?

How did college go from being an exclusive experience to a cultural norm? First, generous federal student-lending policies explain part of the transformation.

Second, the American economy increasingly depends upon jobs that require workers who have high levels of technical and communicative proficiency. Since the 1950s, commensurate with rapid developments in technology and communications, degree-favorable jobs in sectors like technology, health care, and finance have become a greater part of the economy. Simultaneously, largely due to outsourcing and productivity gains, blue-collar, nondegree jobs in sectors like manufacturing and construction have decreased.

A study conducted by economists at Georgetown University found that from 1973 to 2007, America added sixty-three million jobs, but the jobs requiring a high school diploma or less fell by two million.[3] Prior to about the 1970s these jobs formerly paid a wage that would sustain a family, but wages for these jobs today have flatlined, while jobs in white-collar sectors have seen a soaring increase in the average compensation. Starting around 1970, nearly all of the income gains in the United States have gone to those in the upper 50 percent of income distribution—those preponderantly holding college degrees, working in sectors like finance, law, communications, and technology.[4] Seeing this correlation, more Americans are responding to financial incentives and following the money into economic sectors that offer greater earning potential. One sector is not seeing relatively stable and decent-paying jobs filled—skilled vocations, some of which require a degree and some of which do not. As we will explore in detail later in this chapter, skilled labor professions, many of which are culturally perceived to be low-class work, have been neglected.

Third, there is also a social reason that college enrollment has grown significantly. As a result of the financial benefits of having a college degree, and the intellectual and social status it confers on the recipient, there is a growing social stigma in not having a college degree. This, we speculate, may account for much of the "default activity" mentality that Peter Thiel has described. Young people rightly desire more education. But a popular perception has taken root that jobs not requiring a college degree (skilled, hands-on professions like plumber, welder, auto mechanic, and so on) are somehow inferior to more academic, white-collar vocations. Society has wrongly swallowed the notion that these hands-on jobs lack the perceived intellectual or creative cachet of a profession like being a professor, journalist, lawyer, or photographer, and so should be shunned.

Furthering the divide, college has become a class-sorting mechanism. In the postgraduate social marketplace, a college degree is a signaling device that *purports* to indicate a certain level of intelligence, a higher potential for greater income, a certain work ethic, and a commonality of cultural experience that lubricates social interactions and romantic endeavors. In general, people desire these things and want a partner who does also. As Charles Murray has demonstrated in his recent book *Coming Apart*, people with a college degree are more likely than ever before to pair off and marry one another, strengthening their economic hand in the process.[5]

College is also an experimental pond for interests, friends, entertainment, and cultural experiences, both good and bad. Whether one's idea of recreation is playing intramural soccer, joining the marching band, or drinking, college provides an environment for young adults to explore interests and develop relationships with like-minded individuals, largely free from the domestic and parental constraints that previously governed their behavior. Young people throughout history have yearned to get away from their geographic and social roots and all the parental supervision that comes with them. College enables that in ways young adults dream of and parents have nightmares over. The college campus is often a culturally permissive atmosphere of experimenting with drinking, drugs, partying, sex, and sometimes learning. For these reasons and more, young people want to be at college. A four-year, on-campus college education is effectively the modern American *Rumspringa*—a time of discovering what paths to take into adulthood. Whether college should be the default locus for young people to assert their nascent adult identities is another question; the point is that society perceives it as the distinctive place in American life for adult identity formation to occur.

Politicians have also encouraged broad enrollment in higher education. "Tonight, I ask every American to commit to at least one year or more of higher education or career training," said President Barack Obama in his first State of the Union address. "This can be community college or a four-year school; vocational training or an apprenticeship. But whatever the training may be, every American will need to get more than a high school diploma."[6]

Secretary of Education Arne Duncan backed him up in 2012, saying, "I think the most important thing we can do is have young people go to college and graduate."[7] Obama's 2020 College Attainment Goal seeks an increase in the college degree attainment rate from 40 to 60 percent by 2020, including about eight million more Americans ages twenty-five to thirty-four with an associate's or a baccalaureate degree. Currently, the United States sits ninth in the world in percentage of the population with postsecondary education.[8]

Finally, and most importantly, the biggest reason an ever-growing number of Americans are applying for college is that by a variety of measures—as alluded to above—workers with college degrees earn more money than those with only high school diplomas. The total lifetime difference in earnings between college-educated persons and those with a high school diploma has been frequently estimated at about $1 million.[9] The Bureau of Labor Statistics reported that the 2011 median salary for a BA holder was $1,053 per week but only $638 for a high school graduate with no college. Similarly, 2011's unemployment rate for college grads was 4.9 percent but 9.4 percent for high school grads with no college.[10]

Should Everyone Go?

Owing to the reasons listed above, many Americans still think college is worth it. But does that mean everyone should go to college? No. That question is far more complicated. There is evidence that, in the aggregate, the average four-year-degree holder has better economic prospects than someone who graduated only from high school. But that generalization depends on many individual contexts. It may be true in general, but it's not true for many—maybe most—people, certainly not every individual. It depends.

For example, over 40 percent of first-time undergraduates don't graduate within six years of starting college.[11] So while college graduates earn more on average than high school graduates, almost four in ten college students don't even graduate and are left with an incomplete education, holding an ever-growing pile of debt. Twenty, thirty, or fifty years ago one might have rightly argued for nearly universal enrollment in college, but at present, with growing tuition costs, unemployment, and debt, not all students should, or need to, go to college. Furthermore, developments in technology and innovation will radically change the nature of college in the future. (We will discuss these at length later in the book.)

The conventional wisdom that everyone should go to college is wrong and has hurt many students who are now wallowing in student-loan debt, many of whom don't even have a degree to show for it. With 50 percent of recent graduates unemployed or underemployed, it's time we take a more nuanced, careful look at higher education and only encourage it for those who are prepared—financially, educationally, and mentally. Several important qualifiers must be considered. The first is that society has consistently taken the wrong approach to what *type* of college education will best serve students economically. We mentioned that the number of jobs requiring some college is expected to increase in the coming years, making some form of college education a prudent choice for most. This education, however, should not be strictly defined as the four-year bachelor's degree. Although society has largely accepted the four-year degree as a one-size-fits-all approach, the labor market has demonstrated a need for positions requiring credentials like certificates, technical training, and associate's degrees that are not being met. One study conducted by Georgetown University found that by 2018, nearly fourteen million jobs will require more than a high school education *but less than a bachelor's degree.*[12] Similarly, another study done at the Harvard University Graduate School of Education predicted that only one-third of all the jobs expected to be created in the near future will require a bachelor's degree or higher.[13] The study figured that roughly the same amount of jobs, however, will need only a training certificate or an associate's degree.[14] And many of those jobs have a high earnings premium.

In 2012, the Bureau of Labor Statistics identified twenty jobs typically requiring less than a bachelor's degree that had a median salary of $50,000 or more, far above the median annual wage of all professions of about $34,000. These included air traffic controllers ($108,000), dental hygienists ($68,000), and geological and petroleum technicians ($54,000), jobs that won't disappear anytime soon.[15] Many of the jobs on the list were in health care and technology, two fields repeatedly shown to be in the top echelon of fastest-growing economic sectors throughout the next decade.

Figure 3.1. Occupations Typically Requiring an Associate's Degree[16]

Occupation	Median annual wage, May 2010*	Projected job openings, 2010–20	Work experience**	On-the-job training
Air traffic controllers	$108,040	10,200	None	Long-term on-the-job training
General and operations managers	$94,400	410,100	1 to 5 years	None
Construction managers	$83,860	120,400	More than 5 years	None
Radiation therapists	$74,980	6,700	None	None
Nuclear medicine technologists	$68,560	7,500	None	None
Dental hygienists	$68,250	104,900	None	None
Nuclear technicians	$68,090	3,300	None	Moderate-term on-the-job training
Registered nurses	$64,690	1,207,400	None	None
Diagnostic medical sonographers	$64,380	31,700	None	None
Aerospace engineering and operations technicians	$58,080	1,700	None	None

Engineering technicians, except drafters, all other	$58,020	16,800	None	None
Electrical and electronics engineering technicians	$56,040	31,800	None	None
Radiologic technologists and technicians	$54,340	95,100	None	None
Funeral service managers, directors, morticians, and undertakers	$54,330	10,700	None	Apprenticeship
Respiratory therapists	$54,280	52,700	None	None
Geological and petroleum technicians	$54,020	7,000	None	Moderate-term on-the-job training
Electrical and electronics drafters	$53,020	7,200	None	None
Occupational therapy assistants	$51,010	16,800	None	None
Precision instrument and equipment repairers, all other	$50,910	5,500	None	Long-term on-the-job training
Mechanical engineering technicians	$50,110	10,400	None	None

*May 2010 median annual wage for all occupations: $33,840. Wage data are for wage and salary workers only.

**Denotes work experience in a related occupation.

Source: BLS Employment Projections program (projected job openings, education, and training data), Occupation Employment Statistics program (wage data).

The Bureau of Labor Statistics also examined jobs requiring some nondegree (certificate) training, such as aircraft mechanics (median wage: $53,000, with 45,000 openings projected through 2020) and industrial operations supervisors (median wage: $53,000, with 88,000 projected openings through 2020). Clearly, there are many opportunities for better-than-average pay without spending four years at an expensive college.[17]

As a consequence of encouraging students into four-year colleges, skilled trades—professions like auto mechanics, welders, plumbers, and aircraft manufacturing technicians—have been largely neglected as viable career options for high school graduates. For one thing, in the midst of tough economic times, these professions and others similar to them are still in high demand. We cited earlier the decline of blue-collar jobs in favor of ones requiring some college, but these jobs are mostly in lesser-skilled blue-collar areas like manufacturing. In an editorial for the *Washington Times*, Michael Morris, the CEO of American Electric Power, one of America's largest power providers, called for ten million new skilled trade positions in America by 2020. The reason? "A shortage of skilled workers in the future could easily cause unthinkable delays and bottlenecks in American commerce."[18] One survey conducted by consulting heavyweight Deloitte and the Manufacturing Institute, a trade group focused on the viability of the manufacturing industry, found 67 percent of US manufacturing executives saying they are facing a moderate-to-severe shortage of skilled workers, nearly 600,000, to be exact.[19]

Mike Rowe, formerly host of the popular Discovery

Channel show *Dirty Jobs*, traveled the country performing the jobs that few Americans want to do. He told us on our radio show *Morning in America* that over time he realized that Americans aren't filling these jobs because they're repulsive, but because our culture has demeaned the value of hard, dirty work as something inferior to intellectual, white-collar vocations. Rowe testified before the US Senate on the nation's skilled labor shortage, claiming one-third of all skilled construction tradesmen in the state of Alabama alone are more than fifty years old.[20]

In 2009, Rowe penned an open letter to President Barack Obama describing the nation's skilled jobs problem, and in 2012 he sent a similar letter to Mitt Romney, a part of which is included here:

> Today, we can see the consequences of this disconnect [related to the workforce] in any number of areas, but none is more obvious than the growing skills gap. Even as unemployment remains sky high, a whole category of vital occupations has fallen out of favor, and companies struggle to find workers with the necessary skills. The causes seem clear. We have embraced a ridiculously narrow view of education. Any kind of training or study that does not come with a four-year degree is now deemed "alternative." Many viable careers once aspired to are now seen as "vocational consolation prizes," and many of the jobs this current administration has tried to "create" over the last four years are the same jobs that parents and teachers actively discourage kids from pursuing.[21]

No matter how high-tech the economy becomes, elevators will get stuck, toilets will get clogged, and power lines will need repair. Given the dismal state of the economy and the growing skills gap, it's time we redeem these jobs as meaningful, valuable professions worthy of all Americans.

In his book *Boys Adrift*, Leonard Sax interviewed a neighbor, Jeff Donohoe, who owns a lucrative commercial contracting business. Despite the technical competency required for his workforce and the attractive salaries, Donohoe still struggles to find skilled and reliable employees for his business. He runs a program in Maryland where he gives his pitch for the trades to classes of high school students who, in his view, "have no particular interest in going to college." To his dismay, "when you explain that there are good jobs in the trades that don't require a college education, they just give you a blank look."[22]

Donohoe suggests this lack of interest

> starts with the parents, and the teachers. They look down their noses at what they call "blue collar" work. They think we're just digging holes and throwing bricks around. They don't have a clue that modern construction techniques are more high-tech than most desk jobs. . . . It's more like brain surgery than it is building sand castles at the beach. But the parents and the teachers think that if a kid doesn't go to college anymore, that kid's a failure.[23]

Even popular culture has largely moved away from including blue-collar characters as centerpieces of television shows and movies. Where *Home Improvement* and *The Simpsons* celebrated the workaday, blue-collar guy as an everyman's hero, those same characters are scarcely found today. In 2009, Matthew Crawford, a PhD graduate from the University of Chicago who now repairs motorcycles for a living, released *Shop Class as Soulcraft*, a book dedicated to espousing the upside of working with your hands. In an attendant essay for the *New York Times*, Crawford wrote, "The trades suffer from low prestige, and I believe this is based on a simple mistake. Because the work is dirty, many people assume it is also stupid. This is not my experience."[24]

We talked to Chris Herndon, a career electrician in his fifties, who lives in Washington, DC. He had a similar perspective. "It's lack of prestige perceived there," he said. "I feel it in the workplace myself. I'm a WASP, so I've never dealt with racism, but I have experienced people not wanting to get in the elevator with me, asking me not to walk through the lobby, use the restroom, etc. And I might make twice as much money as they do. The perception is I am on the lower strata in society."

He told us that for aspiring electricians seeking to join his union, there is a competitive but free five-year training program in which the trainee earns a salary while simultaneously learning a craft and building a comprehensive knowledge base. "Once you finish you can be in your early twenties making a good salary," he said. From the comfort of his book-lined living room in a tidy brick Capitol Hill row house—the kind interns and young Hill staffers dream of owning once they pay off their student loans—Chris intimated how good he has it: "From what I've seen of the salaries of some of the lawyers in this town, if I worked seventy to eighty hours a week, my salary would be right in the neighborhood. But I'm happy to work forty and come home and enjoy my family."

Statistics confirm Herndon's experience. According to the Bureau of Labor Statistics, in 2011, the mean annual wage for an electrician was almost $53,000 a year, but a master electrician like Chris can earn in excess of $100,000 per year.[25] And Herndon's work is far from boring. He tells us, "I am a skilled laborer, so I'm building things, fixing things, making things work. Lots of people think lights and plugs in the house; they aren't thinking about commercial buildings and lights and gear rooms as big as some houses."

And it's not just electrical work. There are lots of specialized manual-labor jobs that can pull better-than-average incomes. In some cases, far better. One *Wall Street Journal* piece profiled a twenty-five-year-old Australian who has worked in the booming Australian mining industry for the last seven years and currently banks around $200,000 per year for his efforts operating a highly specialized and sensitive drill. "I'm qualified enough now that I'll always have a job," he said.[26]

So as not to rely on raw data or personal testimonies alone, we surveyed the "Skilled Trade" employment section of the Cleveland, Ohio, Craigslist website one afternoon. We chose Cleveland precisely because of its reputation for being economically eviscerated by an exodus of blue-collar jobs. We found forty-one listings for skilled labor/trade positions, with many listings advertising compensation at more than $50,000 per year. We even found ads from employers in Buffalo, New York, and Knoxville, Tennessee, there, trying to mine whatever talent might be elsewhere. Curious, we checked out Buffalo's Craigslist. Sure enough, there were twenty-five ads for skilled labor posted on a single Friday alone, more than Buffalo could boast in its marketing/PR section of hirings for the entire week.

Why then is society pushing the expensive bachelor's degree to the neglect of other credentials that might serve students better? Robert Schwartz, who heads the Pathways to Prosperity Project at the Harvard University Graduate School of Education, blames the four-year-college-for-all mentality.

"Almost everybody can cite some kid who marched off to college because it was the only socially legitimate thing to do but had no real interest," he told an Associated Press reporter.[27]

Susan is the mother of a boy ("Ben") for whom school has generally been boring and irritating. Writing for *Inside Higher Ed*, Susan said school "doesn't seem 'real' to him; it is just stuff that everyone is supposed to do with no point and no consequences other than bad grades, which don't seem real either."[28] But she said that she still feels compelled to send Ben to college. Although she sees that Ben demonstrates a great deal of proficiency for hands-on tasks like aviation and music, she recognizes that "of course he will need a college degree to officially do the work he is already doing so capably."[29]

Based on Susan's perspective, it seems that there is a current moving through the culture that a four-year degree is almost always the best choice for students seeking higher education. Susan lamented society's view on the necessity of a four-year degree for economic success, writing, "I can't help thinking it would be nice if kids like him [Ben] could just leap into the working world without being penalized for their different approach to learning, and be judged instead on the quality of the work itself."[30]

Going back to Peter Thiel's "default activity" theory, it is reasonable to believe that many people who have a four-year degree and are struggling economically were wrongly encouraged to attend a four-year college when community college, technical school, or a certificate program would have been the more appropriate choice. Chris Herndon agrees. "Maybe our parents or our society is not helping people find their best spot to contribute in society," he told us. "We say anybody can do anything, but I don't think that's helpful for a lot of people. I don't want to stifle people's dreams, but on the other hand, you have to say, 'I need to find something I can do well.'"

In short, to us it seems there are simply too many people enrolling in four-year colleges. The economic benefits *tend* to make a four-year degree worth the cost for some of those who have one, but as we have shown, many jobs do not *require* a four-year degree to live a prosperous, middle-class lifestyle. Our friend Charles Murray has discussed this paradox at length in his essay "Are Too Many People Going to College?" Murray writes,

> For the student who wants to become a good hotel manager, software designer, accountant, hospital administrator, farmer, high-school teacher, social worker, journalist, optometrist, interior designer, or football coach, four years of class work is ridiculous. Actually becoming good in those occupations will take longer than four years, but most of the

> competence is acquired on the job. The two year community college and online courses offer more flexible options for tailoring course work to the real needs of the job.[31]

But Murray notes,

> When high-school graduates think that obtaining a B.A. will help them get a higher-paying job, they are only narrowly correct. . . . The economic premium for the B.A. is created by a brutal fact of life about the American job market: Employers do not even interview applicants who do not hold a B.A. . . .
>
> Employers value the B.A. because it is a no-cost (for them) screening device for academic ability and perseverance.[32]

We see that there is an artificial demand for BAs. An expensive, four-year BA rarely confers the skills necessary for most jobs; those skills are learned in training. Rather, employers value the BA because it signals to them what *type* of person they are hiring. Even if the BA were as rare as it was in the 1950s, we doubt employers would stop hiring individuals whose skill set qualifies them for the job.

Preparing Young Americans

If we are to unbind young people from the chains of student debt and convince them there are often better ways to compete in the job market than strictly obtaining a BA, we must equip them to make the right decisions in regard to the level and type of education appropriate for them.

First, the K–12 education system should focus on guiding high school seniors into the postsecondary educational choices best suited to their individual talents and inclinations. A mediocre student who plans to attend a mediocre college to get a piece of paper suitable to employers and to meet girls should be educated by his guidance counselor about the financial advantage to a low-cost associate's degree in a competitive field compared to a $60,000 BA.

Consider a scenario that Murray devised. If a young man considering college is in the 70th percentile in communication skills and average in math but in the 95th percentile in small motor skills, he is more likely to become an excellent plumber, with more income potential, than an excellent middle manager at a corporation, where he will make less. It probably doesn't maximize this young man's earning potential to attend a four-year college. But choosing an educational path cannot be done solely on the basis of testing for aptitude. Intangible considerations, such as the emotional satisfaction derived from the profession, a factor that is hard to disregard, complicate the issue.[33]

The American K–12 system would also do well to look to Germany and promote a secondary education system in which students are guided into the appropriate scholastic or vocational education. Ninety-seven percent of Germans have a high school diploma, but only 33 percent of them go on to college.[34] The best students are placed into academic tracks that will prepare them for traditional undergraduate programs. Those who are average students and primarily interested in education for the economic benefits (and not learning for its own sake—a topic to be discussed later) are directed into high schools that offer hybrid classroom/apprenticeship programs, even for white-collar professions like legal assistants and bank tellers. Students better suited for vocational, blue-collar professions are placed in vocational high schools. This system serves students by helping to coordinate their abilities with the needs of the labor market.

In similar countries, like Austria, Denmark, Finland, the Netherlands, Norway, and Switzerland, between 40 and 70 percent of students are in programs that combine classroom education with vocational training.[35] Moreover, as George Mason University economist Alex Tabarrok has written, there is an additional benefit to vocational education: "[I]nstead of isolating teenagers in their own counterculture, apprentice programs introduce teenagers to the adult world and the skills, attitudes, and practices that make for a successful career."[36]

Another idea that should be entertained at the K–12 level is teaching trades alongside traditional academic subjects. In one version of an ideal school, for instance, every student would be reading Shakespeare on Monday and doing auto repair on Tuesday.

Let's turn to Elliot Stegall, a white, fifty-one-year-old professor of film studies working on his dissertation, now on public assistance. By his own admission, Stegall has spent the last fourteen years ensconced in purely theoretical learning, to his regret. Sitting in a Florida WIC (public assistance to women, infants, and children) office with his family, he gave an interview to the *Chronicle of Higher Education* in which he questioned the usefulness of his degree in the light of an academic and economic climate that doesn't value his skills the way it once did. "As a man, I felt like I was a failure. I had devoted myself to the world of cerebral activity. I had learned a practical skill that was elitist," he says. "Perhaps I should have been learning a skill that the economy supports."[37]

Having a skilled trade would have helped to shield Stegall and his family from the blows of the recession. Additionally, teaching a diversity of both cerebral and manual skills would help break down the ill-considered notion of the financial and social inferiority of blue-collar work and expose students to the underappreciated benefits of manual labor. This is especially true of boys and young men, who are placed in an educational system that often does not consider their biological predisposition for activity and hands-on work.

Says Matthew Crawford, the philosopher-cum-mechanic, "It is a rare person, male or female, who is naturally inclined to sit still for 17 years in school, and then indefinitely at work."[38] Additionally, says Crawford, there is a deep relationship between book learning and hands-on projects:

> If the goal is to earn a living, then, maybe it isn't really true that 18-year-olds need to be imparted with a sense of panic about getting into college (though they certainly need to learn). Some people are hustled off to college, then to the cubicle, against their own inclinations and natural

> bents, when they would rather be learning to build things or fix things. One shop teacher suggested to me that "in schools, we create artificial learning environments for our children that they know to be contrived and undeserving of their full attention and engagement. *Without the opportunity to learn through the hands, the world remains abstract and distant, and the passions for learning will not be engaged.*[39]

Moreover, with a sharper skill set for skilled labor professions upon graduating from high school, Americans could help retake many of these jobs that have been filled by illegal aliens, merely because they have increasingly become "jobs Americans won't do."

Having said all this, the most basic level of the K–12 system must simply do more to better educate its students. A college campus today is seen as the place to complete one's education and gain the knowledge necessary for a successful career (even if it actually isn't obtained there). This wasn't the case fifty years ago; employers still hired high school graduates, and the American economy thrived. But high schools then were better. In November 2012, at a forum sponsored by the Aspen Institute and the *Atlantic* magazine, Microsoft founder Bill Gates commented on the phenomenon that there are many unemployed workers, but employers cannot find qualified people to hire. "Many people want jobs, and there are a lot of open jobs," Gates said. "It is up to the education system to equilibrate that."[40] One organization working to fill the gap between education and the workforce is Project

Lead the Way, a rigorous STEM education curriculum program that trains teachers and equips students in STEM subjects so they are prepared for college and the demands of a modern workforce. Many successful PLTW students go on to college to pursue STEM–related degrees, and some even enter the workforce right out of high school.

Too often today college freshmen and sophomores spend valuable time in remediation for subjects they should have learned and mastered in high school. We need to do more to boost student achievement, especially in the fields of math, science, and writing, where standards have slipped tremendously in the last few decades. By doing so, we can remove the stigma holding back workers without a college degree and help obviate the need for superfluous college education as a minimum requirement for a job interview in a competitive field.

Majoring in Dead Ends

Compounding the problem of too many students in college, too many students gravitate toward majors in which they gain few skills or for which there is little workplace demand. In 2010, the *New York Times* profiled Cortney Munna, a twenty-six-year-old graduate of New York University (NYU) living in San Francisco, struggling to pay down nearly $100,000 in student-loan debt.[41]

Conventional wisdom would hold that a degree from a highly regarded school like NYU would land Cortney a job with a high earnings premium, which would leave her with extra cash to pay down her debt. Instead, she works as a photographer's assistant, making twenty-two dollars per hour. Some of her difficult situation can be ascribed to a crueler job market than usual, but we speculate that her interdisciplinary degree in religious and women's studies isn't distinguishing her from many peers because it is hard for employers to tell what skills Ms. Munna has by virtue of such a degree. Her degree signals that she *may* be able to write well, interpret information, and think critically. But in an age with a huge glut of BAs, so can many other graduates from good, and most likely cheaper, schools.

Munna's story reflects a broader trend in higher education. In recent decades, the number of students majoring in disciplines such as the humanities, social sciences, and arts has increased, while the number of students earning degrees in areas of greatest need has lagged and fallen behind the needs of the labor force.

Consider the findings of George Mason economics professor Alex Tabarrok, who has performed an analysis of graduates in STEM (science, technology, engineering, and math) disciplines since 1985. Tabarrok found that the total number of students in college has risen by 50 percent since 1985.[42] But in the field of mathematics and statistics, there were only 15,496 graduates in 2009, slightly more than the 15,009 graduates of 1985.[43] The same can be said for the fields of microbiology, chemical engineering, and computer science: we graduated more students in those fields in 1985 than we do today. Conversely, found Tabarrok, "in 2009 the United States graduated 89,140 students in the visual and performing arts, more than in computer science, math, and chemical engineering combined, and more than double the number of visual and performing arts graduates in 1985."[44] Ninety-five thousand students walked with a BA in psychology in 2009, more than double the number in 1985.[45] We do not intend to demean these majors, but we wish to illustrate where students are directing their resources and efforts while well-paying and emotionally fulfilling jobs go begging.

Also worrisome is that fewer Americans are filling these available STEM jobs in the United States. Nick Schulz of the American Enterprise Institute has written extensively about the importance of human capital (talent, skill, intelligence, education) in an economy's workforce, particularly in STEM fields. He notes that American workers are lagging behind many international countries in human capital, and these emerging countries are sending their skilled workers to do American jobs. Schulz writes that, according to the Federal Reserve Bank of Dallas, "immigrants accounted for well over 50% of the growth in employment in STEM-related fields between 2003 and 2008."[46] While the US economy values and thrives on immigrant labor, we must do more to cultivate the ranks of American skilled laborers here at home.

STEM jobs, after all, are not just important for their own sake. They also tend to have much higher salaries than jobs requiring a degree in the humanities, arts, or social sciences, like public relations, publishing, government work, paralegal, and entry-level corporate jobs. Many students who are frustrated by their inability to land a job with their BA in the classics or sociology or are weighed down by a mountain of debt would have been wiser to entertain majoring in disciplines for which there is more appreciable employer demand.

STEM jobs are not the only ones for which there is demand; there will be critical needs in the health care, finance, and education sectors in the future. But the decline of STEM graduates especially means that America's global economic competitiveness is diminished. Many STEM majors in college today are on student visas. Too often they take their knowledge back to their home countries competing against the United States, for example, China, India, and Russia.

The problem is that easy loans empower students to pursue degrees that are perhaps more personally interesting and fulfilling to them but have little economic value. To help raise awareness of which majors pay what, students would be best served by being exposed late in their high school years or early in their college careers to detailed data on each major's employment rate a year after graduation and the average salary for each discipline, perhaps as a condition of a school certifying a student loan. PayScale.com, a career service site for workers and employers, has published a comprehensive list of undergraduate majors sorted by earnings. (See figure 3.2.) All but one (economics) of the top twenty majors with the highest midcareer salaries are STEM disciplines.

Figure 3.2. Top Ten Majors by Midcareer Earnings[47]

Rank	Major	Starting Salary	Midcareer Salary
1	Petroleum Engineering	$98,000	$163,000
2	Aerospace Engineering	$62,500	$118,000
3	Actuarial Mathematics	$56,100	$112,000
4	Chemical Engineering	$67,500	$111,000
5	Nuclear Engineering	$66,800	$107,000
6	Electrical Engineering	$63,400	$106,000
7	Computer Engineering	$62,700	$105,000
8	Applied Mathematics	$50,800	$102,000
9	Computer Science	$58,400	$100,000
10	Statistics	$49,300	$99,500

Of course, there is the possibility that encouraging STEM education could one day produce a glut of STEM majors, but for the foreseeable future, this does not appear to be a problem. Moreover, one can major in other disciplines outside STEM fields that have a strong lifetime earnings potential.[48]

Likewise, federal and state governments should consider allocating education resources (specifically, student-loan and grant dollars) preponderantly toward majors that tangibly contribute to the economic good of society. In 2011, Florida governor Rick Scott proposed just that. "If I'm going to take money from a citizen to put into education then I'm going to take that money to create jobs," Scott said. "So I want that money to go to degrees where people can get jobs in this state," he said. "Is it a vital interest of the state to have more anthropologists? I don't think so."[49] In April 2012, Scott signed into law a bill creating an entirely new public university with a focus on producing STEM graduates.

Predictably, Scott's comments were ill received by the former University of Florida president Charles E. Young, who questioned Scott's grasp of the worth of less economically viable disciplines. "It's sheer and utter nonsense," he said. "They have a total lack of understanding about what a university is and what universities do."[50] Young has something of a point: in an ideal education system, restrictions on how dollars are spent would never conflict with the profusion of a particular branch of knowledge; to do so could stifle academic freedom and innovation. But the reality is that many American universities (supported by huge amounts of taxpayer dollars), now considered by students as the de facto place for job training, have churned out many debt-loaded or vocationally uncompetitive graduates, many with majors that have little or no use to employers.

How many colleges or universities offering anthropology majors are needed in Florida? A cursory search we did on our own reveals eleven institutions in the state that offer anthropology majors, almost all of which receive some kind of federal funding. Our opinion is that not all of these programs are needed, and they could be consolidated into one or two great programs at a state or private university without choking off the need for anthropologists (if there is such a need). The degree to which taxpayer-funded university systems allocate majors and degrees should be in sync with the needs of the labor force.

In order to help provide students a better return on investment and keep America economically competitive, some retrenchment of soft disciplines is needed. Universities in China will soon begin abandoning or cutting majors in which the employment rate for graduates falls below 60 percent for two consecutive years.[51] We do not advocate this sort of statist solution, which limits the mission of the university as a place for the free exchange of ideas, but the Chinese method is correctly operating on a principle that every major must be made to defend its existence partly on the grounds of pecuniary return on investment—particularly when discussing the extension of public monies.

Using statistics from PaysScale.com and Georgetown University's Center on Education and the Workforce, *Kiplinger*, which offers personal finance advice and counseling, assembled the worst college majors for a successful career based upon the unemployment rate and median salary for graduates in that particular major.

According to the data, the worst major for economic success in today's current job market is anthropology (Governor Scott may have been on to something). The average unemployment rate for all recent graduates of the top one hundred majors is 6.7 percent (for all graduates with a bachelor's degree, it's 4.9 percent). The unemployment rate for recent anthropology majors is 10.5 percent.[52]

The median income for recent graduates of the top one hundred majors is $37,000 (for all graduates with a bachelor's degree, it's $54,756). The median income for a recent anthropology graduate is $28,000. As *Kiplinger* points out, that's less than the median pay for someone with just a high school diploma.

The second worst is majoring in fine arts. The unemployment rate for recent graduates with fine arts degrees is 12.6 percent, and their average salary is $30,000. Third worst is film and photography majors. Their recent unemployment rate is 12.9 percent, and their median income is $30,000. Photo aficionados, beware; it may be more economically prudent to pursue photography on the side while working toward a more profitable degree.

Fourth worst is a major that's near and dear to Bill's heart: philosophy and religious studies. Bill earned a PhD in philosophy at the University of Texas, but that was decades ago when tuition costs did not stymie future economic success. Today, that's sadly a different story. We would never discourage students from studying philosophy but advise them of the risk they're undertaking. The unemployment rate for recent graduates is 10.8 percent, and the median salary is only $30,000.

Number five may surprise you: graphic design. Thought to be trendy, hip, and an emerging career market, graphic designers are not as successful as many think. The unemployment rate for recent graphic design graduates is 11.8 percent, and their median income is $32,000.

The business community should also have more input into the sorts of workers needed. In Georgia, the Atlanta Chamber of Commerce has taken this initiative in forging a closer relationship with Georgia's universities by starting the Atlanta Business–Higher Ed Council, chaired by Coca-Cola CEO John Brock. The council will try to match the demands of employers with the curricula being taught in Georgia universities.[53]

Dan Nassimbene, a regular *Morning in America* caller who owns an appliance repair business, complains about how difficult it is to find qualified young workers. He gave us some of his thoughts on how to produce the type of worker that he and many other businesses need:

> Any school district receiving federal dollars should be required to provide access to a "trades program" magnet school. This should be a four-year program that provides comprehensive training in the trade of your choice, be it construction, technical, industrial, etc. The educational curriculum within this school should also be tailored to support these students.

What Difference a School Makes

So let's say a high school graduate has evaluated the evidence and decided to attend a four-year college. Every student would love to have the name Harvard or Harvey Mudd on his or her diploma, but the reality is that the vast majority of students end up at colleges with far less name recognition and prestige than those institutions. They want to go to a school where they can get a degree employers will desire. But do graduates of a more prestigious school (which are typically more expensive) really enjoy a greater lifetime earnings premium? In other words, are top-notch schools really worth their high price tag? Or are these schools really just selling academic reputation alone? Should a student attend a more expensive school that has a better reputation or a less-expensive one that is not as well known?

We've already demonstrated that the idea of colleges competing on the basis of magazine rankings and prestige is often very subjective. But this is largely only when we are comparing schools of a similar statistical profile to one another. In truth, it appears that where you go to college makes a difference in your lifetime earnings when comparing the full spectrum of high-performing and low-performing colleges and universities.

In 1999, researchers at the RAND Corporation, Brigham Young University, and Cornell performed a study that tried to answer this question. In an analysis of college graduates of the 1970s and 1980s, their study concluded that "strong evidence emerges of a significant economic return to attending an elite private institution."[54]

For the class of 1982, the best private and public schools had a much higher wage premium to them than other schools, and especially private schools that were (or considered to be) of lesser quality. In essence, the research found that paying a high price for a middling public or private school (privates are generally more expensive than publics) was, in economic terms, not worth the high up-front opportunity cost and actually caused the graduate to *lose* money in the long run. Though the study did not try to identify the cause of why an elite private school delivered a higher wage premium, it appears that in some ways the college prestige machine, in tandem with employer preference for a BA, is working in the way traditionally thought. Employers want to hire applicants who have what is perceived to be the most prestigious education—it is considered a signal of the applicant's intelligence and work ethic. Moreover, as graduates of top institutions rise to the top of their professions, they perpetuate relationships with other similarly credentialed graduates who recognize like-minded talent and will one day have hiring authority.

The findings of the 1999 study seem to be corroborated by a study conducted by Mark Hoekstra, a professor at Texas A&M. In 2008, Hoekstra studied data on earnings from twenty-eight- to thirty-three-year-olds who had attended "flagship" universities—the best public schools in their respective states. His results indicated that white male attendees of the flagship state university had a 20 percent advantage in earnings over those who did not get in, despite having close levels of SAT scores (a generally accurate indication of innate intelligence and ability).[55] Although (or even *because*) those denied admission probably attended another college of slightly lesser quality, their earnings were generally a good bit less than the cohort with a slightly better academic record. It seems the school and its reputation made a difference.

Similarly, in 1996, another group of researchers compared sets of female twins—one who attended "Ph.D.-granting, private universities with well-paid senior faculty and smaller enrollments" (think, for instance Cornell, Georgetown, and Pepperdine), and one who did not. The twin who attended that type of school had "significantly higher earnings later in life" over the one who attended a college that did not enjoy the same characteristics.[56]

These studies suggest that, for what can be a variety of reasons, where you go matters, and students should be apprised of this fact. Just as we should have greater disclosure and visibility for the return on investment (ROI) of specific majors (as we noted earlier), America's colleges or the federal government should publish statistics on postgraduate employment and earnings to help a student determine the value of each school. Although no such mechanism now exists, PayScale.com, an online resource for salary and benefits information, has undertaken an initiative that provides a template for what we would like to see. PayScale has published a list of 1,248 four-year colleges in the United States, with each entry accompanied by data (millions of PayScale users who are also full-time graduates working in the United States) for each school in areas such as cost (four years total) and the average thirty-year return on investment in net dollars. Figure 3.3 lists the ten colleges with the highest ROI in 2012:

Figure 3.3. Colleges Ranked by 30-Year Net ROI, 2012[57]

Rank	College	Type	2011 Tuition (4 years)	30-Year Net ROI
1	Harvey Mudd College	Private: Engineering	$212,900	$1,467,000
2	California Institute of Technology (Caltech)	Private: Engineering, Research	$207,400	$1,417,000
3	Massachusetts Institute of Technology (MIT)	Private: Engineering, Research	$208,100	$1,238,000

4	Stanford University	Private: Research	$220,200	$1,194,000
5	Princeton University	Private: Research, Ivy League	$205,600	$1,163,000
6	Harvard University	Private: Research, Ivy League	$210,400	$1,115,000
7	Dartmouth College	Private: Research, Ivy League	$212,000	$1,102,000
8	Duke University	Private: Research	$210,900	$1,060,000
9	University of Pennsylvania	Private: Research, Ivy League	$212,800	$1,001,000
10	University of Notre Dame	Private: Research	$203,500	$978,800

Note: These figures are in 2012 dollars.

The PayScale rankings analyze the thirty-year net ROI by calculating the earnings differential between a college and a high school graduate (widely assessed by experts to be about $1 million over a lifetime) and then balancing that against the tuition costs and average earnings of the attendee of the particular university being assessed. The system also factors in the school's graduation rate, since not all college attendees graduate.

For example, from PayScale.com, "a school with an 80 percent graduation rate, $1,000,000 earnings differential for graduates, and $200,000 in weighted costs would have a $640,000 net return on investment."[58]

PaysScale specifically compares the earnings differential for the thirty-year net ROI of the median pay for a bachelor's degree at a particular college or university versus the thirty-four- to thirty-six-year earnings of a high school graduate in the seventy-fifth percentile (an average of high school students).

PayScale notes that by using this specific ROI calculation, about two hundred institutions of higher learning have a negative thirty-year net ROI. PayScale explains, "This means the typical person who graduates from these schools would not make their money back if they were in the 75th percentile or above of high school diploma-only earners. In other words, the return for these schools is lower than the investment of attending and thus the ROI is negative."[59]

Put it a different way: In pure financial terms, students might be better off investing their tuition money in stocks and bonds rather than in a degree from one of our nation's many colleges.

Therefore, from figure 3.3, we see that PayScale's findings are consistent with the studies we cited earlier indicating the earnings premium of an elite, private school. Private, elite colleges occupy all the places in the top ten. Moreover, that institutions with a focus on high-earning STEM disciplines occupy the top three slots gives weight to the idea that major is also determinative of earnings. The evidence is further confirmed when we see only two public institutions (Colorado School of Mines and Georgia Tech—both STEM heavy) in the top twenty.

One recent addition stands out. In September 2012, PayScale reported that graduates of the South Dakota School of Mines and Technology now make on average more than Harvard graduates: $56,700 to $54,100.[60] These numbers reflect the massive boom in oil and natural gas resources in mineral-rich states like North and South Dakota. Although this boom might last only a few decades, it shows the importance of STEM education and a university system that is in sync with the demands and needs of an ever-changing workforce, particularly as it relates to energy.

Of course, it is hard to control some factors about the data. Wealthier students, who have more financial and parental resources at their disposal, are primed to do better in life anyway. And from these data alone, it's easy to see how hyper-earning professionals like top DC lobbyists, New York financiers, or Silicon Valley techies bring up the numbers. But on the whole it seems that there is a positive return for attending an elite, private school. Is there a commensurate loss in attending a below-average private school, as one study suggested? Let's look at what PayScale thought to be the bottom ten colleges:

Figure 3.4. Colleges Ranked by 30-Year Net ROI, 2012[61]

Rank	College	Type	2011 Tuition (4 years)	30-Year Net ROI	Annualized ROI
1239	Marywood University	Private	$165,900	-$161, 000	-7.8%
1240	University of Montevallo	Public	$100,700 (out of state)	-$161,000	-12.3%
1241	Jackson State University	Public	$117,900 (out of state)	-$163,000	-12.3%
1242	Nazareth College of Rochester	Private	$151,800	-$166,000	-12.3%

1243	College of the Ozarks	Private	$104,200	-$176,000	-12.3%
1244	Meredith College	Private: Liberal Arts	$142,000	-$179,000	-12.3%
1245	Medaille College	Private	$130,100	-$184,000	-12.3%
1246	Judson University	Private	$151,100	-$186,000	-12.3%
1247	Seton Hill University	Private	$160,200	-$186,000	-12.3%
1248	Savannah College of Art and Design	Private: Art, Design, Music	$176,900		-12.3%

Consistent with the 1999 study conducted by the RAND Corporation et al, eight of the ten colleges on PayScale's list with the worst thirty-year ROI are unspectacular private colleges, with a *negative* lifetime ROI. That means by paying full tuition to Meredith College for four years, for instance, you will make $179,000 less over thirty years than the thirty-four- to thirty-six-year earnings of a high school graduate in the seventy-fifth percentile. In other words, it is more likely you would be better off financially if you graduated from high school and did not pay full tuition to attend Meredith College. For whatever reasons, either many Meredith students drop out, or a Meredith degree has not distinguished itself in the eyes of employers to the extent that it justifies $36,000 per year in tuition cost.

Now let's identify some colleges that, in strictly financial terms, seem to be a good value for the average undergraduate (figure 3.5). Stanford has unquestionable value, but most students will never get in, plus it has a very expensive tuition cost. What are some schools with a lower tuition cost but high long-term return? First, let's assume that most students will not gain admission to top-tier private or public colleges—we'll arbitrarily cross off the Ivies, plus some other Gotta Get-Ins, a term invented by *Atlantic* writer Gregg Easterbrook to describe the schools that wealthy parents in the Washington, DC, area were dying to send their children to. That means no Amherst, Berkeley, Caltech, Chicago, Duke, Georgetown, Johns Hopkins, MIT, Northwestern, Pomona, Smith, Stanford, Swarthmore, Vassar, Washington University in St. Louis, Wellesley, or Williams.

Second, no specialty schools such as engineering or maritime training schools, even though the data show a terrific return on investment for places like Montana Tech and the Colorado School of Mines. Let's set the "good value" parameters as colleges costing under $125,000 for four years but statistically producing a lifetime premium of $300,000 or more. Remember, PayScale.com's methodology is only counting the ROI of a bachelor's degree, so the returns associated with a graduate-level or professional degree don't apply here. Also, pretend that everyone attending that given school pays the full price tag, so no considerations of financial aid (loans or grants) are factored in. The result is almost entirely a few dozen public, mostly large universities with in-state tuition.

If we consider Georgia Tech an outlier (it has a mostly STEM focus and has very competitive admission), and if we purely consider the regnant consideration that most families face when paying for college—minimizing short-term cost while maximizing long-term return—then UC–San

Diego seems to be the holy grail of college value according to PayScale. The average student can expect to pay $107,000 for a BA there but earn slightly more than $647,000 over thirty years on his investment.

Figure 3.5. Best Value Schools, 2011
(Bennett-Wilezol Methodology)
(All tuition is in-state dollars unless otherwise specified.)

College	2012 ROI Rank	2011 Tuition Cost	30-Year Net ROI
Georgia Tech	17	$82,340	$836,000
UC–San Diego	40	$107,000	$647,100
University of Virginia	49	$85,310	$620,900
University of Illinois–Urbana–Champaign	50	$104,900	$620,000
Texas A&M	58	$86,980	$568,900
Virginia Tech	60	$85,740	$551,600
William & Mary	61	$87,570	$544,800
California Polytechnic–San Luis Obispo	62	$93,490	$542,700
UCLA	67	$111,300	$537,400
University of Maryland	70	$91,420	$518,000
University of Michigan	71	$96,430	$517,100
Rutgers University–New Brunswick	72	$112,900	$515,900
UC–Irvine	80	$106,700	$483,300
University of Washington	86	$86,690	$471,400
Brigham Young University	87	$75,290	$468,200
University of Texas–Austin	90	$97,550	$464,200
UC–Santa Barbara	96	$118,100	$448,200
UC–Davis	97	$114,500	$447,700

Stony Brook University (out of state)	98	$110,800	$445,400
Purdue University	103	$88,460	$420,400
SUNY–Binghamton	106	$77,430	$416,700
Miami University (Ohio)	107	$114,900	$415,400
Clemson University	109	$99,970	$409,200
University of Connecticut	112	$96,070	$401,800
SUNY–Binghamton (out of state)	115	$107,500	$392,600
University of Wisconsin–Madison	117	$86,050	$390,400
University of Massachusetts–Lowell	128	$90,780	$366,900
Penn State University	129	$117,200	$364,900
UC–Boulder	132	$103,900	$361,600
James Madison University	133	$79,560	$360,500
Cal Poly–Pomona	134	$82,500	$360,400
George Mason University	135	$83,200	$356,500
University of Florida	138	$68,410	$351,000
The College of New Jersey	139	$106,400	$350,100
North Carolina State University	155	$73,440	$329,700
Texas Tech	156	$81,890	$328,000
Rutgers University–Camden	177	$113,800	$306,900
University of Delaware	179	$85,470	$303,700
Auburn University	182	$84,110	$302,900

The most troubling part about this calculation is that these forty colleges make up only 3.2 percent of all the colleges on PayScale's list.

Too many schools cost more than the ones in figure 3.5 and give students an even or negative return on their investments. Consonant with the findings of the 1999 RAND et al paper, many of these schools with subpar returns are private schools that are expensive, but of lesser quality or name recognition than the top tier (Ivies and other Gotta-Get-Ins). Most of these schools appear elite. They tout a campus glossed with nice facilities, avant-garde academics, or competitive sports teams. But in the long run, the student is paying more to get less.

There has been some criticism of PayScale's methodology because it doesn't take into account the other indicators of financial success, like a student's GPA, SAT scores, and intellect. Furthermore, there are many variables among colleges themselves, like faculties, students, and campus ethos, which can affect one's future financial success.

In some ways this criticism is correct; where you earn your diploma doesn't automatically guarantee your future salary or earnings. Enrolling in a top school doesn't guarantee you a well-paying job any more than enrolling in a subpar school instantly relegates a student to his parents' basement. An acceptance letter to an elite university is not a golden ticket to a six-figure salary. Work ethic, diligence, and intellect are still some of the strongest indicators of personal success. America has successful Meredith College graduates and unsuccessful Harvard dropouts.

But to ignore the PayScale data entirely is to ignore an important piece of the financial equation. That is because the returns associated with an elite college, or, for that matter, any college, do take into account, in an aggregate sense, students' GPAs, intellects, and ambitions, as well as the name of the college or university on their diplomas.

For example, when we read that Stanford's ROI is approximately one million dollars more than Barnard College's, we acknowledge that different students with different sets of skills attend Stanford and Barnard College. But taken in their entirety, and calculated over thirty years, their return on investment is a reflection of an accumulation of individual sets of talents, intellect, and motivation. If you graduate from Stanford, it means you were good enough to get into Stanford. Once there you are exposed to their motivated and talented students and faculty and network of business connections. And the cumulative effect of all that over many years is substantial and what separates the elite schools from the middle-of-the-rung schools. A degree from Stanford has a better statistical chance of fattening your paycheck than a degree from a middle-of-the-road college, but that's because you were probably smart, able to grit your teeth, complete the rigorous coursework, and hunt down a well-paying job after graduation.

In short, PayScale's ROI list is a broad snapshot of the median salary graduates of each college have earned in the past and an analytical prediction of what they are likely to earn in the future. But it is ultimately a set of statistical data and projections, not an oracle. PayScale's data is probative and useful, but its not the final word. Its most helpful use for students may be in illustrating the general ethos of an institution, respect of a specific school's program by employers, and the type of students and professors you are likely to surround yourself with if you attend that respective school.

Using PayScale's data, we did an analysis of schools whose four-year tuition cost was $200,000 or more, but whose thirty-year ROI was less than $200,000, in other words, schools that may be perceived as prestigious (reflected in the high short-term cost) but in reality do not live up to the highly unscientific "bang for your buck" criteria that consumers use when buying *anything* (figure 3.6). Here's what we found:

Figure 3.6. Most Overvalued Schools, 2011
(Bennett-Wilezol Methodology)

School	2012 ROI Rank	2011 Tuition Cost	30-Year Net ROI
Barnard College–Columbia University	324	$215,200	$192,800
UC–Riverside (out of state)	328	$202,400	$189,500
Colby College	338	$206,400	$184,700
Vassar College	348	$210,800	$182,500
Franklin and Marshall College	406	$206,800	$149,600
Skidmore College	458	$210,800	$130,400
Drew University	459	$215,300	$130,200
Rhode Island School of Design	470	$220,900	$124,600
University of Denver	470	$208,400	$124,600
UC–Santa Cruz (out of state)	489	$208,400	$117,200
Smith College	524	$209,400	$100,300
Farleigh Dickinson	533	$200,300	$98,040
Oberlin College	697	$214,200	$44,980
Simmons College	741	$201,100	$35,110
Rollins College	766	$208,600	$29,590
Mount Holyoke College	905	$209,100	$-1,420

Bryn Mawr College	963	$207,400	$-16,400
Berklee College of Music	1079	$212,400	$-50,100
Art Institute of Chicago	1207	$214,300	$-103,000

Several factors account for why people pay so much money for these schools.

First, students are allured by the prestige associated with many of these "name" schools. Five schools on the list (Barnard, Vassar, Smith, Mount Holyoke, and Bryn Mawr) are in the Seven Sisters cohort—a group of liberal arts colleges considered to be among the best in the country outside the Ivy League. But the data suggest that you have a statistically small chance of recouping your investment anytime soon if you go there. Why would a "prestigious" school's graduates not be able to cash in? Our hypothesis is that students at these colleges are preponderantly majoring in liberal arts and social sciences, which, as we have demonstrated, have higher unemployment rates and lower lifetime wage premiums. At Bryn Mawr, for instance, the most popular majors, as reported by *U.S. News and World Report*, were English literature, foreign languages, biology, and psychology.[62] Even then, the Bryn Mawr name has trouble redeeming a major that doesn't pay.

Second, college is an investment that hopes for a high return, but it is also a retail purchase. Families with more resources at their disposal (or students with a greater willingness to take higher amounts of debt) may have few qualms paying high out-of-pocket costs for luxuries like Barnard's Manhattan locale, Oberlin College's idiosyncratic creative community, or the Florida sun of Rollins College. But for families and students who want to optimize their resources and/or avoid student loans, it makes no sense to pay money for these schools when others will, statistically speaking, provide a much better return.

Let's say that, hypothetically, pure dollar return is a student's sole concern in choosing a college. Why would she pay for a Bryn Mawr degree when numerous other schools will statistically provide a much higher earnings premium? She wouldn't. But if the same student, regardless of expense, so desired her college experience to be at a small, all-women's college with a prestigious classics program (what Bryn Mawr offers), then she might be more comfortable subordinating the idea of pure return on investment to those retail considerations and paying extra. But for most students, who see a college degree mostly as a means to economic ends, the choice is clear. In fact, according to UCLA's Higher Education Research Institute, of more than 190,000 incoming freshman surveyed at 283 four-year colleges in 2012, 88 percent said their reason for attending college was to get a better job—the single most common response and the highest percentage ever recorded since the survey began in 1966.[63]

Other Factors to Consider

However, there is still one major gap to be filled in considering the value of college. In particular, we have not yet allowed for how much a college degree matters in light of an individual's personal characteristics. Is it possible that a college degree actually adds no earnings premium to an individual, but a person's qualities such as talent and motivation are the sole determinants of career success? To put this another way: What happens to the talented individual who does not attend college? Are his or her lifetime earnings worse off without a college degree or better off without the burden of debt?

In 2011, PayPal cofounder and venture capitalist Peter Thiel tested this thesis for a few extremely talented individuals and started the 20 Under 20 Thiel Fellowship, a program that brings together the most enterprising students younger than twenty and offers them a $100,000 grant to skip college and explore their own research and entrepreneurial ideas. Under the tutelage of investors, scientists, and like-minded industry tycoons, students are able to develop connections, court investors, and promote their businesses on a level that Thiel says colleges cannot provide. In May 2011, Thiel announced the first twenty-four Thiel Fellows (the applicants were so extraordinary Thiel had to add four more spots). So far, the results have been impressive.

Eden Full, nineteen, who founded Roseicollis Technologies to improve solar energy technology in developing countries, recently won the Staples-Ashoka Youth Social Entrepreneur award and $260,000 to continue her efforts.[64]

Andrew Hsu, twenty, started a company called Airy Labs to develop mobile and tablet social learning games for children. Airy Labs reportedly launched with $1.5 million in venture capital funding.[65]

According to James O'Neill, head of the Thiel Foundation, more than ten of the fellows have started their own companies, and one of them released his own product on the market.[66] It appears that Thiel's recruits are so gifted by nature that they don't need college. Doing so might actually hinder their intellectual progress, since they are already by nature in the rarest intellectual air.

We should remember that by definition the vast majority of college-bound students do not possess the extraordinary cognitive gifts that these students do. Thiel's fellows are certainly outliers, but perhaps their success outside higher education says something about the system at large. If the best and brightest students don't need a college degree to succeed, perhaps elite universities are not so elite after all. Perhaps higher education isn't so high after all. Perhaps it should be more accurately called middle-of-the-road education.

Former White House economist Alan Krueger considered this question of personal determination vs. environment in a 1999 study. He and fellow author Stacy Dale analyzed the returns of attending an elite college. The findings were consistent with those of other reports we have cited. Students who attended places like Yale, the University of Pennsylvania, and Swarthmore in 1976 were earning an average of $92,000 in 1995—$22,000 more than students who entered Tulane, Denison, or Penn State the same year.

However, when Krueger sampled students who were admitted to the most selective private colleges but decided to attend only a "moderately selective" one, he found that their lifetime earnings "varied little, no matter which type of college they attended." The one exception was students from disadvantaged backgrounds, who saw a significant jump in lifetime earnings.

In publishing his results, Krueger concluded that the student contributed more to his success than the school he attended:

> That you go to college is more important than where you go. Find a school whose academic strengths match your interests and that devotes resources to instruction in those fields. Recognize that your own motivation, ambition and talents will determine your success more than the college name on your diploma.[67]

But what about an individual who doesn't attend college at all? To our knowledge, no study has been published that charts the career progress of individuals who were qualified to enroll but decided to forgo college out of high school. There are certainly the well-known success stories of millionaire and billionaire college dropout geniuses like Bill Gates, Steve Jobs, and Mark Zuckerberg. But again, they have their own genius streaks that defy the usual means of education. They are closer to the Thiel Fellows than the rest of us.

For a closer perspective relating to the average college-bound student, we interviewed Sarah Danaher, a twenty-seven-year-old full-time wedding photographer in Washington, DC. Danaher never went to college but still affords an apartment (with a roommate) on Capitol Hill and a car payment. She occasionally travels. As the owner of her own business, Ampersand Photography, Danaher works hard, not just in photographing events, meeting clients, and networking, but doing the back office work of handling promotions, bookkeeping, and taking care of tax requirements.

Most would assume a college degree is necessary for this work. But talking to her, we found it impossible to draw a distinction about whether she is college educated or not.

Danaher gave us her thoughts on why she chose not to go to college and her perspective on why people do go:

> Culturally, it's assumed that if you don't go to college you don't have a chance, or you're not living up to your true potential. A person who has no college but willingness to learn and work hard has unlimited ability to achieve, but people who don't think can get stuck in the idea they must go to college. I was raised with entrepreneurial mind-set, and my parents saw a strength and told me what I could do. Education wasn't ignored, but viewed as means to an end, not end to itself.
>
> After high school, I didn't want to go to college at the time. At some point I briefly contemplated it, and the idea of debt was the biggest, scariest thing I could think about it. I'm one of nine, so my parents paying for it wasn't really an option. And it isn't the mind-set of my parents to give things for free anyway. And I didn't know what I was or what I wanted to do. So it made no sense for me to go to four-year college to get education I didn't know I wanted. It's asking an awful lot of an eighteen-year-old to decide on what they want to do with their life. People don't decide on a major until a couple years in. College is a very valuable thing, but only if it contributes value to the rest of their life. The only part of me that regrets not going is feeling not as prepared for my job as I could be. The

learning curve was steeper in the beginning. If I could do it over, I would possibly consider going to school for business if I could get it for free or very reduced cost.

I don't feel economically but feel socially disadvantaged in DC because this is where people don't ask 'where did you go?' but 'where did you do your undergrad?' But the older and more established I get, the less I feel a stigma of not having a degree. Four or five years ago when I was looking for jobs I felt frustrated because I didn't have that one piece of paper, even though I was qualified in my job experience and general competency. A lot of what is 'normal' is really stupid.

Danaher's experience may be emblematic of the more motivated and driven young men and women bypassing college, but in the end, we really can't know for sure all the trends of what happens to people of varying backgrounds, incomes, and educations who decide not to attend college.

Considering the Military

Before we conclude this chapter, we must note that one branch of collegiate institutions is almost always worth the investment: the military. Institutions like the Air Force Academy, West Point, the Naval Academy, and the many other military schools around the country are truly schools of higher learning. Not only are the academics sound and the financial aid benefits well worth the investment, but also the character development and skills training are invaluable for life. If you are thinking of joining the military through one of these academies or colleges, your investment will be well worth your time and money. These institutions are models of higher education, not of just the mind but of the body and the soul.

In this chapter we've spoken largely about the financial worth of a college education. However, attending college isn't all about money. There is indeed value in learning for its own sake. There's no doubt that colleges are still teaching things, but what are they teaching? Moreover, are students actually learning worthy things? In our next chapter, we'll explore the contemporary academic side of the American university to see if it's worth the cost or the four-year commitment.

FOUR

The Lower Side of Higher Ed

We've discussed many aspects of the price of college. But there is also a dimension that ought to be every bit as important as the financial return, if not more so. We are speaking, of course, about the fundamental purpose of college—education—and whether the value of the material taught in the classroom justifies the high cost of higher education today.

There are several questions to be asked: What exactly are students learning today? Is higher education preparing students for gainful employment? Is it training skilled, competitive workers? Is the education itself valuable on its own merits, and does it shape students' intellectual and moral horizons in ways that prove beneficial to them and the public interest?

To start, let's establish the mission of the university and how well or poorly universities are fulfilling that mission. The English word *education* comes from Latin. It combines the verb *ducere* (lead/draw) with the prefix *e* (out of). The intent of education is to lead someone or something forth or draw something out. But what does this mean in the world of higher education?

The author William James had the right idea in his essay "The Social Value of the College-Bred." "The best claim that a college education can possibly make on your respect, the best thing it can aspire to accomplish for you, is this: that it should *help you to know a good man when you see him*," wrote James.[1] And James warned that all too often, "to be a college man, even a Harvard man, affords no sure guarantee for anything but a more educated cleverness in the service of popular idols and vulgar ends."[2] Note that James is discussing both intellectual and moral development. To that end, in his view, the purpose of college is to help turn the mind and the soul toward what is objectively true and good in the world.

America's first institutions of higher education understood the relationship that James described. The first college in America was Harvard, founded in 1636. Eventually, William and Mary in Virginia came along, then Yale. Virtually all of these schools placed a priority on religious education (indeed, Yale was founded in response to a perception that Harvard was teaching the Bible unfaithfully) and the classical education of ancient Greek and Latin—the backbone of all Western learning.

The value of the instruction was not just in teaching the intellectual concepts that the Bible or the ancients impart. Young minds were forced to concentrate on—and apply to their lives—the sources of learning that have formed the basis for Western standards of truth, beauty, and conduct. As the apostle Paul wrote to the Philippians, "Whatever is true, whatever is noble, whatever is right, whatever is pure, whatever is lovely, whatever is admirable—if anything is excellent or praiseworthy—think about such things."[3] From ancient times until fairly recently, universities built their educational philosophy upon Paul's words.

In earlier times, when there was much more uniformity of curriculum in higher education (and fewer people in college), students could feel more comfortable about majoring in liberal arts and still securing employment. This is not just because college degrees were much rarer but also because the educational philosophy of higher education had not yet gravitated toward seeing college as a mere means (training) toward an end (a job).

In eighteenth- and nineteenth-century Britain, for instance, virtually every young man privileged enough to attend school studied Latin beginning at age seven or eight and Greek from ten or twelve. If he continued on to college, it was usually to read more Greek and Roman authors and other classic works in preparation for a career like the clergy, law, government, the academy, or medicine.

It seems counterintuitive that the liberal arts formed the core education for so many different careers. But the British Empire, a massive polity successfully administered around the globe for generations, got along fine with men who never studied sociology, public administration, or communications. Instead, their ideas of sociology came from Tacitus's ethnography of the Germans, public administration from Plato's *Republic*, and communications from memorization and recitations of Cicero's *Catilinarian Orations*.

The story goes that someone once asked a Greek don, "'Why study Greek?' He said you should study Greek not only because it is the immediate language of the Holy Ghost, but its study also leads men to positions of great dignity and emolument." More than a decade of close study of the Western canon often produced individuals who didn't question whether their degree qualified them for a job. And they were equipped with knowledge that has been historically instrumental to intellectual and moral flourishing no matter what their vocation.

Well-Cultivated Mediocrity

In contrast, there is a great misconception today among students that the purpose of college is to prepare the student for a career. This idea clashes with a traditional Western intellectual philosophy of education that finds its roots in the Greek Socratic tradition and, by extension, the medieval university. "Universities are not intended to teach the knowledge required to fit men for some special mode of gaining their livelihood," the political philosopher John Stuart Mill told students at the University of St. Andrews in 1867. "Their object is not to make skillful lawyers, or physicians, or engineers, but capable and cultivated human beings."[4]

Ideally, students would take James's, the apostle Paul's, and Mill's words to heart and choose a major purely on the basis of intellectual edification or satisfaction. But the decision of choosing a major is made more difficult by the modern idea that college is also a place to acquire job skills.

Many still adhere to choosing a major purely on the basis of intellectual and emotional benefits. Flash back to NYU graduate Cortney Munna, whom we mentioned earlier. Even with nearly $100,000 in student-loan debt, Munna seems comfortable with her liberal arts NYU education that nets her twenty-two dollars an hour. She described her interdisciplinary degree in women's studies and liberal studies, as "by no means a vocational education, but . . . academically rigorous . . . [it] helped prepare me for innumerable future careers."[5] Likewise, an editorialist in *USA Today* wrote,

> The bottom line is, you should choose a major you love, even if you're not sure how it will help you in your career search. If you can defend what you're passionate about (and still have the skills to do the jobs you're applying for), your employer will see that passion. I'm not a journalism major, but my studies in classics have given me a different perspective in my editorial experiences and have never hindered my job search.[6]

As philosophy and classics majors ourselves, we agree.

But Munna's and the editorialist's views have shortcomings. It's good that the *USA Today* columnist hasn't had a job search hindered by an uncompetitive major. But there are many baristas at Starbucks who can't say the same. Majoring in art history may afford you priceless, detailed knowledge of Michelangelo's *David*, but little in the way of career opportunities or earning power relative to other professions in finance, health care, or oil and natural gas services. If that trade-off is acceptable to you, go to it. But in general, you should carefully choose a major by considering what you like to study, what the employment and earnings prospects are for that major, how much the education will cost, and what sort of mind and sensibility the major will form. It may be a violation of the educational orthodoxy of James, the apostle Paul, and Mill to consider your education in terms of economic returns, but it would be irresponsible of us in this day and age to construct arguments while disregarding this view. The cost of pursuing higher education is too high not to. We are taking things as we find them.

The purpose of this book is not to debate the efficacy of higher education. Whether you see college primarily as a place to secure a job qualification or a program to shape the human person and cultivate virtue, the reality is that the modern university has proven in many cases indifferent to cultivating the minds and souls of its students. While espousing a rhetoric that proclaims higher education, the seriousness of study and meaningfulness of content itself belie lower impulses and motivations, leaving many students unprepared for life or morally adrift. Let's catalog the ways that many American colleges are failing their students.

Slipping Academic Standards

First, students enrolled in American universities are generally not demonstrating adequate academic performance. College leaves many of them both uncultured and unemployable. In general, students are not being challenged, nor are they obtaining tangible knowledge under the low standards that already exist.

Part of the reason is that many students attending colleges shouldn't be there in the first place. An essay appeared in the *Atlantic*, written by an adjunct English professor who identified himself only as "Professor X." Having spent a decade teaching writing at lower-tier American universities, filled with "students whose applications show indifferent grades and have blank spaces where the extracurricular activities would go,"[7] Professor X is convinced that there are too many students in college, and that many are there just to obtain a piece of paper that will make them employable for jobs on a police force, in a hospital, or in municipal government. Many of these students do not appreciate its original purpose—learning for its own sake. Says Professor X:

> My students take English 101 and English 102 not because they want to but because they must. Both colleges I teach at require that all students, no matter what their majors or career objectives, pass these two courses. For many of my students, this is difficult. Some of the young guys, the police-officers-to-be, have wonderfully open faces across which play their every passing emotion, and when we start reading "Araby" or "Barn Burning," their boredom quickly becomes apparent. They fidget; they prop their heads on their arms; they yawn and sometimes appear to grimace in pain, as though they had been tasered. Their eyes implore: *How could you do this to me?*[8]

Most of us have from time to time sat through courses in which we grit our teeth at the material. But in addition to not being interested in the material, says Professor X, many students are actually *incapable* of doing the work assigned. He continued his comments:

> A few weeks into the semester, the students must start actually writing papers, and I must start grading them. Despite my enthusiasm, despite their thoughtful nods of agreement and what I have interpreted as moments of clarity, it turns out that in many cases it has all come to naught.
>
> Remarkably few of my students can do well in these classes. Students routinely fail; some fail multiple times, and some will never pass, because they cannot write a coherent sentence.[9]

Professor X realizes many of his students are uninterested in the business of learning, and therefore it is not surprising that they struggle. Their instincts are not bent toward intellectual inquiry. Mary Grigsby, a sociologist at the University of Missouri, did a study on college life in 2009. One student described his approach to schoolwork thusly:

> I hate classes with a lot of reading that is tested on. Any class where a teacher is just gonna give us notes and a worksheet or something like that is better. Something that I can study and just learn from in five [minutes] I'll usually do pretty good in. Whereas, if I'm expected to read, you know, a hundred-and-fifty page book and then write a three-page essay on it, you know, on a test let's say, I'll probably do worse on that test because I probably

> wouldn't have read the book. Maybe ask the kids, what's in this book? And I can draw my own conclusion, but I rarely actually do reading assignments or stuff like that, which is a mistake I'm sure, but it saves me a lot of time.[10]

Where do you put the *sic*? The same student told Grigsby, "I can get out of here with a 3.5 [GPA] but it doesn't really matter if I don't remember anything. . . . It's one thing to get the grade in a class and it's another to actually take something from it, you know."[11] Yes, we do.

What this inability or unwillingness to understand college-level material reveals is that the universities have dumbed down their standards and expectations. Universities graduate more than a million students each year, but how and why is this happening if students aren't actually taking something from class? The answer is that colleges have succumbed to the same malady as that found in K–12 education, what President George W. Bush described as "the soft bigotry of low expectations."

Students aren't being academically challenged in the ways that are appropriate for students in college. Daniel de Vise, the education reporter for the *Washington Post*, interviewed Ashley Dixon, a sophomore at a school in the DC area. "I was expecting it to be a lot harder," said Dixon, twenty. "I thought I was going to be miserable, trying to get good grades. And I do get good grades, and I'm not working very hard."[12]

Dixon's experience of getting good grades without pushing herself is backed up by a recent study done by Professors Stuart Rojstaczer and Christopher Healy. In a study of grades given to 1.5 million students from more than two hundred schools from 1940 to 2009, they found that today, on average, As represent 43 percent of all letter grades, an increase of 28 percent since 1960 and 12 percent since 1988. Additionally, Ds and Fs constitute less than 10 percent of letter grades in American universities today.[13] And if you believe that the data are skewed by less competitive schools with less capable students, think again. Rojstaczer and Healy found just the opposite: "Prestigious schools have, in turn, continued to ramp up their grades . . . private colleges and universities give, on average, significantly more A's and B's combined than public institutions with equal student selectivity."[14]

In 2002, the American Academy of Arts and Sciences conducted a similar study and found that in 1966, 22 percent of Harvard students graduated with As. By 1996, that number was 46 percent, and by 2002, 50 percent, with eight in ten students graduating with some kind of honors.[15] Harvard has some of the brightest students in the country, but even that does not account for such precipitous grade inflation over time.

Without high standards for achievement, students are spending far less time than ever hitting the books. Two economists at the University of California at Santa Barbara produced a paper in 2010 titled "Leisure College, USA." They found that compared to their predecessors of 1961, who spent forty hours a week studying and learning in class (making school essentially a full-time commitment), college students today spend a combined twenty-seven hours a week learning in class and studying outside it.[16] The authors of the book *Academically Adrift* corroborated this, finding that students only did, on average, between twelve and thirteen hours of work outside class per week.[17]

This can't just be ascribed to students choosing easier majors, enrolling in less competitive institutions, or working more to help pay for college. The UC–Santa Barbara professors found that declines in workload "fell for students from all demographic subgroups, overall and within every major, for students who worked and those who did not, and at 4-year colleges of every type, degree structure and level of selectivity."[18] Instead, the college culture has changed so that leisure activities have assumed a much larger role in student life. Commensurate with the decline in workload, "Leisure College, USA" found that time devoted to leisure activities increased nine hours per week between 1961 and the 2000s.[19] Detached from serious academic commitments, many students are devoting more time to free time, whether it be fraternity or sorority life, student government, sports, booze, or video games.

It should be no surprise that as students have grown accustomed to being rewarded for mediocrity, they are learning less than ever before. In reflecting on the dismal attitudes toward learning in Professor X's classroom, we turn toward a landmark study published in 2011 by sociologists Richard Arum and Josipa Roksa titled *Academically Adrift*. In the course of studying 2,300 students for several years, Arum and Roksa observed in 2011 that 45 percent of students in their study made "no statistically significant gains in critical thinking, complex reasoning, and writing skills" in their first three semesters in college. Forty-five percent of students developed no real skills in their first three semesters in college! And this is not just a problem that can be ascribed to freshman-year social adjustments. Arum and Roksa report that "students are likely to learn no more in their last two years than they did in the first two, leaving higher education just slightly more proficient in critical thinking, complex reasoning, and writing than when they entered." This, too, shouldn't be surprising, when one-fifth of seniors report coming to class "frequently" unprepared, and one-half report they have never written a paper more than twenty pages in length.[20]

Why is this kind of underachievement happening on college campuses? There are several reasons. First, there seems to have arisen a kind of tacit understanding between students and professors when it comes to grades and workloads, something higher education analyst Murray Sperber has referred to as a "non-aggression pact."[21] Knowing that students prefer to spend more time having fun than studying, professors are more comfortable awarding good grades while requiring a minimum amount of work. In return, students give favorable personal evaluations to professors who desire to be well received by students as a condition of preserving their employment status. Indeed, the popularity of the student evaluation, which began in the 1970s, has had a pernicious effect. Especially as reviews freely accessible to anyone get posted on sites like RateMyProfessors.com, students can build an academic career around which professors will be the most unchallenging.

Rebekah Nathan, an anthropology professor at a large state university, did an undercover assessment of campus life by posing as a freshman student for a year and writing about her experiences in her book *My Freshman Year.* Here are some of the comments from course evaluations she examined:

> Take Professor Jones, the man to see when you need an "A." Don't take 302 with Smith because you can't understand what he wants you to know and he doesn't give As. "I loved 101. It was sooo fun! And sooo easy!" Need to boost your GPA? Take 242.[22]

This is the academic side of the Bennett Hypothesis: Allow schools access to free money, and they will increase their fees to increase their revenues. Allow students to set their own academic agendas, and many will choose the easiest course work available. Not always, but often enough to skew the entire system.

Seeing the academic results such back-scratching has produced, it is laughable that, according to one survey, 99 percent of professors said that critical thinking was a "very important" or "essential" goal of undergraduate teaching.[23] Professors must take a stand and hold their students to far higher standards.

With the commercialization of higher education today, exhibited by a university like High Point that we described earlier in the book, many colleges and universities are more concerned with their bottom lines than their students' academic well-being. With millions of easy student-loan dollars up for grabs, there is little or no financial incentive for colleges and universities to get in touch academically and risk losing students and those students' financial aid dollars. It would be against the interest of the faculty and administration. So rather than treat their students like stockholders—offering them the best possible product for their investment—they treat them like a mass production assembly line, moving them through the academy as quickly as possible and capturing as many loan dollars as possible. If professors and school administrations won't hold their students to higher academic standards, students and parents should demand better.

Teachers Who Don't Teach

Second, in the modern university system, there is a disproportionate relationship between professorial prestige and teaching responsibilities. In the 1950s, the French-born American professor Jacques Barzun noticed that professors were starting to shift their teaching workloads onto adjuncts and graduate students. "The highest prize for the teaching profession is: no teaching," he wrote. "For the first time in history, apparently, no scholars want disciples."[24] When I (Bill) was teaching an Introduction to Philosophy course at Boston University in the 1970s, my department chairman routinely thanked me for my "sacrifice" in teaching an introductory course in philosophy for undergraduates.

The prevailing orthodoxy among many of today's senior professoriate is that they should be allowed to concentrate on researching topics of their own choosing, to the exclusion of teaching duties. But these established professors are the ones who often know the most in their fields and have the greatest ability to inspire students to take an actual interest in the subjects they are studying. More professors should seek to emulate instructors like Michael Sandel at Harvard, who fills large lecture halls every year with his masterful course on justice, and the late Harold Rood of Claremont McKenna College, whose grasp of American politics and warm decency made deep and positive impressions on many of his students.

Yet many, if not most, tenured professors spend their time engaged in their research, with teaching considered a chore. We remind you of a stat we presented in chapter 2: 80 percent of the faculty at UT–Austin teach fewer than half the students. Why such unproductivity? Schools like to attract top faculty to enhance their reputations in the academic community. Princeton wants to have better scholars than Yale, who wants to have better scholars than Harvard, and so on. To attract students and research dollars, schools feel compelled to draw star professors. Since there's inherent scarcity in celebrity professors, the schools have to compete with one another in ways previously unknown—including paying teachers not to teach.

In lieu of teaching, many professors build up their professional identities in ever specialized and arcane areas of published scholarship. But what contributions to knowledge are being made? As it turns out, most academic work is ignored. Worst of all is the humanities. From 1980 to 2006, 21,674 pieces of scholarship (books, articles, dissertations, and so on) were published on William Shakespeare. Poor William Faulkner is neglected by comparison, with 3,584, and Charles Dickens had only 3,437 studies devoted to him.[25] How much of this do people actually read? Very little.

As the number of colleges and professors has exploded since

the 1960s, so has the amount of scholarly research. But there are indications that much of it is read less than ever. Consider what some university presses are saying. An editor of the Harvard University Press told the *Chronicle of Higher Education*, "In my experience, monographic studies in the humanities, and I definitely include history here, whether written to win tenure or later in a career by established giants in the field, now usually sell between 275 and 600 copies, no matter how good they are."[26] And of course, even if copies are purchased, nobody has any idea how often they are being read, if ever.

And it's not just the humanities encountering this fate. According to a study by *Science* magazine, only 45 percent of the articles published in the 4,500 top scientific journals were cited within the first five years after publication.[27] Many of these are no doubt graduate students trying to obtain their spot at the research dollar buffet, or buying into the prevailing mind-set of aspiring scholars, which holds that you must publish original research to get hired or get tenure. But with so many different articles in so many publications, academic reputations are now more fleeting and insular accomplishments than ever, and many times only perfunctory gestures performed to bolster one's CV. In the words of R. R. Reno, writing in *First Things*, "Who remembers more than one in twenty award-winning academic books even of the last decade? Visit used bookstores. It's a sobering exercise in the high mortality rate of reputations."[28] Let's reduce the pressure on scholars to publish and instead link tenure and pay with teaching quality, rather than academic output.

Additionally, when professors do get tenure and more

freedom to perform research, they get expensive. Full professors, according to the American Association of University Professors, make an average of more than $113,000 per year.[29] Many of these professors do not teach, but students must still receive instruction. In order to save money, schools have begun using adjuncts (part-time professors) more than ever before. In 1960, 75 percent of professors were full-time, tenure-track professors. Today, only about 27 percent are.[30] At Penn State, a value state school, 55 percent of faculty are adjuncts; and 40 percent of the faculty are adjuncts even at pricey, elite Brown University.[31] Adjuncts, many of whom have second jobs, are usually notoriously poorly paid, often making less than minimum wage when preparation time is factored in. Since many adjuncts are graduate students hoping to eventually be hired as full-time professors, they, too, are quick to adopt a pedagogy that ensures praise from students.

The Price of Underachievement

Third, student underachievement has grown because parents paying for college expect tangible results for sending their sons or daughters off to an expensive school. If a school gets a reputation for not producing enough students with degrees, parents (particularly those capable of paying full tuition out of pocket) will send their kids (and dollars) elsewhere. Not wanting to lose precious dollars, administrators are lax in enforcing academic standards. Nor are schools eager to disclose their results. In 2007, the University of North Carolina–Chapel Hill voluntarily adopted the College Learning Assessment Test to gauge what students there were learning. Unfortunately, the results have never been made public, despite many other schools who use the CLA doing so. UNC probably didn't like what the results of the CLA had to say.[32] In sum, colleges have no financial incentive to impose more stringent academic standards, and the consequences of such decisions have been dismal. Does anyone know a real, serious student who studied and tried to do the work and flunked out of college?

The Faulty K–12 System

Such underachievement also indicates that the K–12 system has failed to teach the skills that truly prepare students for higher education. If students enroll in college en masse because they feel they cannot get a good job with only a high school education, they should at least be prepared to do college-level work.

Professor X's students taking freshman-level English 101–102 courses probably just graduated from high school the previous summer or are adults who have been in the workforce for some time, seeking a degree to advance in their careers. How can the American K–12 system rightfully describe itself as educating students when it produces adults who, in Professor X's words, cannot construct a proper sentence? Far from being led forth, they are being strung along by the same low-standards approach in high school. Why are students who cannot write a "coherent sentence" enrolled in a college class? Many students who are chronically averse to challenging material in college are probably the type we have identified who would be better served by attending community college or obtaining other vocational training. Instead, the devaluation of a high school education and the social pressure of having a college degree have produced students who have not placed themselves in the ideal educational circumstance.

Additionally, the K–12 system is simply not graduating students with skills that will allow students to compete in the working world. Consider the 1895 high school examination graduation questions of Saline County, Kansas. Here are some questions sampled from a high school examination in a rural part of America at the end of the nineteenth century:

> Find the interest of $512.60 for 8 months and 18 days at 7 percent. Find bank discount on $300 for 90 days (no grace) at 10 percent. What is Punctuation? Give rules for principal marks of Punctuation. Who were the following: Morse, Whitney, Fulton, Bell, Lincoln, Penn, and Howe? Describe the process by which the water of the ocean returns to the sources of rivers. How would you stop the flow of blood from an artery in the case of laceration?[33]

Each of these questions intends to equip the average graduate with knowledge that will allow him or her to prosper in the probable workplace environment of the time. All of the questions are relevant to the tasks of the day: banking transactions, knowledge of geographic features, and how to write clearly. Our K–12 students should similarly be expected to demonstrate the same levels of skill in mathematics, writing, and civic education that will make them competitive in the modern economy.

Unfortunately, a high school education is now mostly seen as functionally useless and educationally passé. The poorer-performing students do not learn the skills that employers demand, and the better-performing students are in a hurry to enter college, knowing that employers offering good jobs generally do not entertain the high school diploma as a qualifying credential on its own merit.

A recent ad by the Target Corporation illustrates this phenomenon. The ad (which is, in fairness, very touching) shows a montage of video clips featuring students exuberantly rejoicing upon reading their college acceptance letters. Then a white screen with text appears: "Every kid deserves this moment. Great schools can get them here. Target is on track to give $1 billion to K–12 education by 2015." The inference is that K–12 education must be strengthened so that students can succeed and then go to college, where they will learn what they *really* need. It's a noble impulse. But it is indicative of how K–12 is wrongly viewed today—a mere stepping-stone to higher education and not a place where students should learn what they need to know to be immediately competitive in the workforce.

Consider that in September 2012, the College Board reported that SAT reading scores for graduating high school seniors hit a four-decade low; just 43 percent of test-taking students were college ready.[34] Spending on K–12 education has approximately tripled over the past fifty years, and results are getting worse, not better. Until K–12 education improves dramatically, there is only so much room for improvement in higher education. The crime here, beyond the squandering of public dollars, is the waste of time we inflict on children. Twelve years of education are compulsory, and many kids have nothing to show for it afterward. In a previous generation they would have been ready for life, a job, and a family. Today college students are ready to exasperate their instructors in remedial English and math classes before they drop out with an average of $23,300 in debt.

For those who will go on to college, appreciation for learning and the development of critical-thinking skills must be restored in K–12 education. Without both, students will have progressively less internal motivation or background knowledge to succeed in a college classroom.

Consider the state of American history—our very worst subject. The 2010 National Assessment of Educational Progress reported that only 12 percent of our nation's high schoolers had an adequate understanding of the nation's past.[35] Not having gained the proper understanding of American history in secondary schools, college students form the impression that its study is distant, difficult, and irrelevant. "We're raising young people who are, by and large, historically illiterate," author David McCullough told the *Wall Street Journal.* "I know how much these young people—*even at the most esteemed institutions of higher learning*—don't know. It's shocking."[36]

Consequences of Low Academic Standards

With such a miserable grasp of students' knowledge at the K–12 level, we shouldn't be surprised at the abundance of remedial course work available, and often required, at America's colleges. To have remedial classes at an institution of *higher education* is oxymoronic at its ironic best and, at worst, defeats the purpose of what and whom college is for.

Most remedial education takes place in community colleges, and according to one estimate by the Community College Research Center, nearly 60 percent of all students in community college took a remedial education course in 2009.[37] We strongly encourage more students to consider community college over a four-year college as a pathway to career success, but we question why so much remedial learning is happening even at the nation's community colleges. It illustrates the social and economic pressure to obtain a college degree, as well as the failure of K–12 to produce individuals with skills.

Derron Bowen, a math professor at Broward College in Florida, where 67 percent of first-year students needed remedial work in 2008, remarked on how the K–12 system has failed students in his class. "How were they allowed to go through?" Bowen asked. "I'm thinking, 'If I could have been teaching you back when you were 6, 7, you would be a powerhouse today.'"[38] One community college student told the Associated Press that he wished he could enroll in a type of apprenticeship program in lieu of community college to get his degree in criminal justice. "College is not for me," said Daniel Paz. "It's something I have to do, but if there was another way, then I'd be doing something else."[39]

But it's not just community colleges that offer remedial courses. Some 20 percent of all freshmen enrolling at *four-year* universities in 2008 were forced to take a remedial course.[40] In most cases, these are students who should have considered community college or a trade school. We don't offer this distinction arbitrarily. Graduation rates for students who started in remediation are horrible. Fewer than one in ten students who require remediation graduate from community colleges within three years, and little more than one-third complete bachelor's degrees in six years.[41] Better K–12 schools will help save states and students money and effort that are not being spent effectively on remedial education.

This is a significant concern. There are several consequences of graduating college students who have not learned much, if anything.

First, graduates are put at a disadvantage in the job market. Mark Cuban, the billionaire technology entrepreneur and NBA owner, has made clear how badly employers want qualified employees, regardless of where they went to school:

> As an employer I want the best prepared and qualified employees. I could care less if the source of their education was accredited by a bunch of old men and women who think they know what is best for the world. I want people who can do the job. I want the best and brightest. Not a piece of paper.[42]

Most employers would agree with Cuban. It's not the piece of paper that matters; it's what an applicant knows, can do, and is willing to do.

Unfortunately, although many have degrees, the data indicates that college students have accomplished very little academically that signals workplace preparedness to employers. A 2011 survey of one thousand hiring managers conducted by the Accrediting Council for Independent Colleges and Schools found how dissatisfied employers are with the quality of college graduates these days. Only 16 percent said that applicants are "very prepared" with the knowledge and skills they would need for the job. Sixty-three percent said applicants are "somewhat prepared," and another 21 percent said applicants are "unprepared". Fifty-four percent of hiring decision makers reported that the process of finding applicants with the necessary skill and knowledge set is difficult.[43]

The *New York Times* reported on Gabriel Shaoolian, a chief executive of a Web-design company who was advertising ten openings. His company could not find enough highly qualified people with technical backgrounds. "If you're a professional developer, Web designer or online marketing specialist, you can pick the company you work for," Shaoolian said. "There is a shortage where demand severely outstrips supply." But Shaoolian hasn't hired anyone because most applicants were unqualified. "It was catastrophically bad," he said. Not able to find adequate full-time help, Shaoolian started to hire freelance contractors located outside the United States. "Greece may be struggling with their economy, but their developers are phenomenal and they are in high demand," he said.[44]

The other major consequence of college student under-achievement is the gradual diminishing competitiveness of American students in the global workforce. Let's refer again to Shaoolian's Web-design business. He was forced to hire foreign workers because American graduates didn't have the skills he needed.

In 2011, I (David) got to know Gengchao, a Chinese graduate student studying at George Washington University. Gengchao's field was economics, but that seemed easy compared to his fellow Chinese students, who were all in programs like physics, statistics, supply-chain management, and chemical engineering. The Chinese education system may have significantly less capacity for innovation than the American system, but it has rightly prioritized the highly transferable and lucrative skills that will make college graduates attractive to employers the world over—STEM fields.

I asked Gengchao what he scored on the math portion of the Graduate Record Exam (GRE). He smiled bashfully. "Eight hundred," he said. A perfect score. American students are simply not competing in ways that are distinguishing themselves from their foreign counterparts.

In February 2011, in a meeting with Silicon Valley's biggest entrepreneurs, President Barack Obama asked Steve Jobs, then CEO of Apple, what it would take to make iPhones in the United States rather than China. Jobs replied that those jobs aren't coming back. "Apple executives believe the vast scale of overseas factories as well as the flexibility, diligence and industrial skills of foreign workers have so outpaced their American counterparts," reported the *New York Times*, "that 'Made in the U.S.A.' is no longer a viable option for most Apple products."[45] This indictment of American education and the labor force it produces should be a wake-up call.

Classic Disciplines Not Being Taught

STEM jobs are critical for breathing life into the American economy, but we realize not everyone has a natural capacity or intellectual interest for excelling in those fields. Furthermore, as we stated at the beginning of this chapter, education is essentially the task of developing the soul and the mind. As I (Bill) recall hearing Patricia Albjerg Graham, dean of the Harvard Graduate School of Education (1982–91), say, to paraphrase, education is the nurture and enhancement of the wit and character of the young. We paraphrase what John Locke wrote in the 1600s about the purpose of education: "'Tis virtue we aim at, hard virtue, and not the subtle art of shifting." The economy and human flourishing in general require students who will be able writers, speakers, teachers, and decision makers, but without the proper character training as well, their education is incomplete.

In the pre-World War II era, this was usually accomplished through the teaching of the classic works of Western civilization's literature, history, philosophy, religion, art, and music.

Think the fruits of the Bible, Homer, Virgil, Aquinas, Shakespeare, Locke, Mozart, Brahms, Michelangelo, the

Declaration of Independence, Abraham Lincoln, and Charles Dickens. As a result, the universities produced individuals who usually appeared something like William James's "good man," conversant in the principles of thought that shape our identities as human beings, citizens, men, and women. Through the dissection of the Great Books, symphonies, paintings, and historical accounts, students learned how to think critically about abstract topics and express those thoughts in writing. Further, the lessons learned from the material itself could be applied to daily situations and serve as reference points for moral and intellectual conduct.

How Well Are America's Colleges and Universities Doing This Today?

Though some universities still teach many of the Great Books and attempt to educate the soul, the process today is far different from the approach of the pre-1960s university. As political and cultural liberalism came to dominate the American university in the 1970s, so the instructional approach suffered. Liberal scholars, informed by a relativistic worldview, increasingly reinterpreted "texts" from any number of vantage points, thus entrenching a hermeneutic in the universities that can broadly be defined as *postmodern*. This largely meant approaching texts from the perspectives of historically underrepresented identity groups like feminists, nonwhite minority groups, and homosexuals. As a consequence of adopting these views, the reputation of the

Great Books suffered, as many liberal scholars dismissed the output of dead white males as variously sexist, elitist, imperialist, bourgeois, ethnocentric, racist, selfish, and solipsistic. If the greats weren't discarded entirely, liberal academics developed counternarratives to describe the great works. In this way, colleges pay lip service to the tradition of the great disciplines and great thinkers by teaching them in the classroom, but do so in a way that emphasizes idiosyncratic and ideologically contorted understandings of the material.

Unsurprisingly, academic relativism followed the intellectual and moral contortions of modern humanities scholars. A modern English department, for instance, might ascribe Japanese comic books the same artistic significance as *Hamlet*. In the rush to embrace continually novel academic disciplines, material fundamental to Western thought and experiences is discarded. In 2012, Peter Berkowitz of the Hoover Institution noted that political science majors at Yale, Princeton, Stanford, and Berkeley could receive a BA without any study of the *Federalist* papers, the essential commentary on the American Constitution written by James Madison, Alexander Hamilton, and John Jay in the 1780s. You wouldn't expect chemistry students to be unfamiliar with the periodic table. Why should students of government at the best universities in America be unfamiliar with one of the most foundational texts of the American republic?

The reason the *Federalist* is neglected, says Berkowitz, is that "the progressive ideology that dominates our universities teaches that the *Federalist*, like all books written the day before yesterday, is antiquated and irrelevant." Additionally, says Berkowitz, "in the misguided quest to mold political science to the shape of the natural sciences, many scholars disdainfully dismiss the *Federalist*—indeed, all works of ideas—as mere journalism or literary studies, which, lacking scientific rigor, can't yield genuine knowledge."[46]

With this in mind, it's not surprising that since 2007, at least four well-respected American universities—the University of Virginia, the University of South Carolina, Wake Forest University, and Arizona State University—have offered a course on the bizarrely behaved pop star Lady Gaga. Yet none of these schools made a course in US history mandatory for graduation.[47] UCLA has offered the course Queer Musicology, which teaches students how "sexual difference and complex gender identities in music and among musicians have incited productive consternation."[48] For the privilege of taking "Queer Musicology," California residents living on campus pay nearly $32,000 per year ($54,000 per year if they are from out of state).[49]

The biggest casualty of academic relativism has been the Core Curriculum, the systematic familiarization of our Western tradition of learning. As I (Bill) said in my Harvard University 350th anniversary address in 1986, higher education usually gives a mere "symbolic nod" to the idea of a core curriculum, but it usually amounts to a "Chinese menu" of selecting courses—mixing and matching whatever catches the student's fancy.

In 2009, the American Council of Trustees and Alumni (ACTA) surveyed one hundred colleges of varying characteristics. ACTA found that "almost half" did not require a college-level math course, 90 percent did not require students to take a survey course in American history or government, and only two required a basic course in economics.[50] A different study by the National Association of Scholars found that only one in seventy-five schools required a course in Western civilization, compared to nearly half in 1964.[51] In a dismal summary of its findings, ACTA wrote that, "The general education requirement has become virtually anything goes."[52]

When relativistic scholars are loathe to teach the basic body of knowledge that has historically constituted a general education, our students are often offered courses laden with—to put it bluntly—nonsense. ACTA found that at one college, students were allowed to satisfy a literature requirement with a course in "Bob Dylan." At another, Floral Art took care of natural sciences.[53] The universities' tradition of teaching "the best that has been thought and said,"[54] as nineteenth-century poet Matthew Arnold put it, is slipping away.

Minds Narrow and Wasted

The modern university prides itself as a bastion of free thought, unencumbered by various intellectual constraints. It celebrates itself as the home of tolerance and diversity. Yet many universities are institutions of a narrow-minded political and societal attitude, often promulgated by the faculty and the administration. Often the university, to quote Harold Rosenberg, is a "herd of independent minds."[55] As has been well documented, the majority of public and private universities are left leaning, both culturally and politically. There is an obvious lack of intellectual diversity within the ranks of higher education. If students are investing their or their parents' livelihoods in college, they should know the intellectual climate they are investing in.

Consider the combined results of two surveys—one published by the American Enterprise Institute and another by the journal *Academic Questions*—that polled professors in the University of California system about their political affiliation. As we can see from figure 4.1, professors in the social sciences and humanities who identified as Democrats vastly outnumbered those who identified as Republicans.

Figure 4.1. Political Affiliation of Professors[56]

School	Field	Ratio of Democrats to Republicans
UC–Berkeley	Sociology	17:0
UC–Berkeley	Political Science	28:2
UC–Berkeley	English	29:1
UC–Berkeley	History	31:1
UC–Berkeley	Psychology	26:1
UCLA	History	53:3
UCLA	English	29:2
UC–San Diego	Politics	27:0
UC–San Diego	History	26:1
UC–Santa Barbara	English	21:0
UC–Santa Barbara	History	28:1

A study conducted in 2007 by Neil Gross and Solon Simmons surveyed faculty from 927 schools, asking respondents to state their political orientation. About 62 percent declared themselves as being to some degree liberal, with another 18 percent identifying as moderate. Almost all of these moderates, however, voted for John Kerry in the 2004 election, compared to 54 percent of self-identified moderates in the general public.[57] *The Daily Princetonian*, Princeton's student newspaper, found that a total of 157 Princeton University faculty and staff members donated directly to the 2012 presidential candidates, with only two of those donations going to Gov. Mitt Romney. The total dollar amount of donations directly to Obama exceeded $169,000, while the donations to Romney amounted to exactly $1,901.[58]

Likewise, the Young America's Foundation analyzed who had been invited to be the key commencement speakers at America's Top 100 Colleges, as listed by *U.S. News and World Report*. It found that seventy-one of them were liberals, compared with only ten conservatives.[59]

Naturally, the views of the faculty are often implanted in their classrooms. One survey conducted by ACTA in 2004 at fifty selective colleges found 49 percent of students claiming they've had professors who frequently inject their political views in class, even if it is irrelevant to the material, and another 46 percent said that they've had professors who frequently use class time to promote their political views.[60] These views are often standard liberal perspectives proffered by Noam Chomsky or the late Howard Zinn. At the University of Pennsylvania, for instance, dozens of faculty members signed a statement of solidarity with the Far Left Occupy Wall Street movement.[61]

When political activism supplants legitimate intellectual inquiry, the university is failing a host of stakeholders. Public universities use taxpayer dollars for unintended purposes. A uniformity of thought and a paucity of differing opinions do not equip students to be informed participants in our democracy. When students realize that some professors desire concurrence with their own political views over demonstrations of critical thought and expression, students' work suffers. As the National Association of Scholars has written, they prioritize the ends of scholarship over the means of learning. Also, students' intellectual inquiry is stunted. They become ensconced in their own conceptions of the world, which, to their detriment, go unchallenged.[62] In this, the true mission of the university is undermined.

Sadly, all of this has been happening for decades. As distinguished professor and cultural commentator David Gelernter has documented extensively, the ranks of academia became flooded with liberals beginning as a consequence of the cultural and sexual revolutions of the 1960s. Conservatives naturally tended to lean toward businesses and churches, while liberals took to the academy and arts. I (Bill) have firsthand knowledge of the liberal establishment and its modus operandi stemming from my long career in higher education and government. When I was teaching at the University of Wisconsin in the 1970s, I saw the members of a seminar in advanced ethics, led by the professor, raid a broken soft-drink machine during a break and steal twenty cans of soda. I told them that what they did was wrong and that the deliveryman might be forced to pay for the shortfall out of his own pocket. The professor of advanced ethics was unmoved, and he reconvened the seminar for further elaborations of ethical dilemmas. So much for practicing what you preach or teach. In the 1980s, when I encouraged colleges to crack down on drug usage, some in the academy criticized me for sounding like a "small-town PTA president." Putting politics aside, students and parents should be fully cognizant of where and how their valuable tuition dollars are being spent. They should ask themselves, Is this product worth the risk of thousands of dollars of debt? Is this worth investing four years of my life and finances?

Higher education has become exorbitantly expensive and inefficient, in part, because of a lack of accountability and pressure from students and taxpayers. As Heather MacDonald has written, even as California's higher education budget withers on the vine, UC–Berkeley found $194,000 to pay its "vice chancellor for equity and inclusion." That's four times the starting salary of an assistant professor. And while UC–San Diego lost star cancer researchers to Rice University and eliminated MA programs in electrical and computer engineering, it added a diversity requirement that prizes "a student's understanding of her or his identity," especially focusing on "African Americans, Asian Americans, Pacific Islanders, Hispanics, Chicanos, Latinos, Native Americans, or other groups" through the "framework" of "race, ethnicity, gender, religion, sexuality, language, ability/disability, class or age."[63]

Bruce Bawer, an author and literary critic who happens to be gay, rejects the rise of identity studies in his new book *The Victims' Revolution: The Rise of Identity Studies and the Closing of the Liberal Mind*: "Identity studies sum up everything that's wrong with the humanities today. . . . Kids don't learn anything other than to think of themselves as having been wronged by capitalism, by the West, by America, by white men."[64]

Bawer explains the historical and cultural consequences of immersing millions of our college students in such identity studies:

> And with every kid who emerges from college possessing a diploma—and an idea of America derived not from the values of the Declaration of Independence and the Constitution but from the preachings of identity studies—the American miracle fades a bit more into the mists of history.[65]

The rise of identity studies on college campuses has helped make *tolerance* and *diversity* the great mission of the universities. These expressions of political correctness are the intellectual mission of the university. When the sensitivities of different groups becomes a greater priority than intellectual inquiry, academic freedom becomes limited. For instance, a student at Indiana University–Purdue University Indianapolis was declared guilty of racial harassment merely because he was reading a book that *celebrated* the defeat of the Ku Klux Klan in a fight with Notre Dame students in 1924. Some university employees complained that the book was racially insensitive just because it featured a picture of a Klansman on the front cover. At the University of Wisconsin–Madison, a vice provost for diversity and climate encouraged students to disrupt an event in which the speaker voiced opposition to racial preferences.[66]

Even many liberals realize how convoluted this sort of thinking can be. George Will profiled Greg Lukianoff, "a graduate of Stanford Law School who describes himself as a liberal, pro-choice, pro-gay rights, lifelong Democrat, who belongs to 'the notoriously politically correct Park Slope Food Co-Op in Brooklyn' and has never voted for a Republican 'nor do I plan to.'"[67] Lukianoff is the head of the free-speech advocacy group FIRE (Freedom for Individual Rights In Education), whose mission is to defend individuals unfairly constrained in their First Amendment rights on campus. Although Lukianoff would not be confused for being a conservative anytime soon, he understands the necessity of preserving the academic freedom to express unpopular, controversial, and politically distasteful opinions.

If the public knew how their tax dollars were being spent, surely they would be up in arms over how the university has failed to develop the moral habits of its students. Take, for instance, one of the modern inventions of the academy: the coed dorm. The *Journal of American College Health* found that 42 percent of students living in coed dorms binge drink each week, compared to only 18 percent of non-coed residents. Almost needless to say, the study found binge drinkers do worse in school, sleep less, and disrupt other students more. The study also reported more sexual partners and higher rates of pornography usage for students living in coed situations. According to one of the researchers, who controlled for a self-selection process (for example, religious students choosing to live in sex-selective dorms), "there was still something unique about living in a coed dorm that was associated with risk-taking."[68]

Some of the most vivid examples of the university's moral unorthodoxy and detachment from reality appear in an article by Jeffrey Goldberg in the *Atlantic*. Goldberg reviewed the policies of several universities that addressed what to do if an "active shooter" (deranged killer) should penetrate the short-sighted "gun-free zones" that colleges label themselves. Of course, a sign declaring a "gun-free zone" will make no difference to a madman with intent to kill. But don't tell the universities. The University of Miami advocates counteracting any incident by "improvising weapons" and "yelling." West Virginia University encourages that students "act with physical aggression and throw items at the active shooter." The list of recommended items is risible: "student desks, keys, shoes, belts, books, cell phones, iPods, book bags, laptops, pens, pencils, etc." Goldberg's conclusion about why these policies are in place is accurate: "The existence of these policies suggests that universities know they cannot protect their students during an armed attack." Our purpose here is not to impugn universities for restrictive gun laws, although we would welcome a change in that regard. Our purpose is to highlight the fantasyland the universities inhabit in thinking that symbolic gun-free zones will prohibit violence or that throwing belts and pencils will hinder the carnage of a man with a gun.[69]

Is this learning environment worth the investment of $50,000, $100,000, or $200,000? Consumers make highly informed decisions when they're buying a home: Is the neighborhood safe? Are the schools good? Where are home prices headed for this area? Can I get a better deal somewhere else? If students and parents are investing almost as much money into a college education as a home, they should make equally informed and careful decisions.

Thankfully, some within the ranks of higher education are beginning to look out for their consumers. John Garvey, the president of the Catholic University of America (CUA), has taken a truly bold stand against the dorm culture of drunkenness and promiscuity. In March 2011, he announced that all dorms at CUA would eventually revert to single-sex residence halls. Although recognizing how unpopular the choice was among students, Garvey was persuaded by the statistics to make the move, saying simply in an op-ed in the *Wall Street Journal*, "our students will be better off."[70]

The examples above illustrate in large part why many of today's institutions of higher learning fail in their most basic responsibility—cultivating learning, skills, and critical thinking. Too many of today's college students know more about sex, drinking, and partying than they do about history, literature, math, or science.

Too many of our college students are wasted, literally and figuratively. Regardless of whether the mission is preparing students for a job or developing their minds, too many colleges are failing.

FIVE

With Eyes Wide-Open

Despite the parlous economic, intellectual, and social condition of higher education we have documented, the situation is far from hopeless, and there are many bright spots in places of excellence and success. Many students do graduate each year and find good jobs. Some of America's students are still some of the best-educated graduates in the world. In the classroom, not every professor is a doctrinaire liberal, and not every student is subject to social ostracism or subpar grades for expressing unpopular political views. Not every student is only putting in twelve hours of homework per week—just ask architecture, engineering, or classics majors. Not every college student binge drinks or is sexually promiscuous. Some, even many, learn, grow, and eventually prosper.

But, as we have also documented, the financial viability and quality of college are imperiled. While the expansion of federal loan programs allowed many students to obtain a degree that was for them previously financially prohibitive, the easy availability of this money now often saddles students with more debt than they can handle. Where academic freedom abounded to allow professors to pursue scholarship without a backlash from administrative politics, it now is a license to teach frivolous subjects or brainwash students. And where the dorm was devised as an experiment to build campus cohesion, it has been an enabler of the hook-up culture, the effects of which can be pernicious.

We have addressed these problems and offered solutions in piecemeal fashion throughout this book, but the purpose of this chapter is to reiterate what can and should be done to produce a generation with less debt, more knowledge, and more noble character.

Step Out of the College Rut

The most fundamental reform that should be made is abandoning the idea that a four-year college education is the appropriate or even necessary choice for everyone. Many who embrace the view that every American should have a four-year college education rightly highlight the strong positive correlation between a bachelor's degree and lifetime earnings—frequently estimated to be more than $1 million. Similarly, they also correctly point out that college graduates have higher employment rates than those who graduated only from high school. But this does not mean that a four-year college is the right choice for all or that every four-year college is the right choice, period.

It is important to remember that the data are true only in the aggregate. From a perspective that emphasizes the statistical probability of a certain level of financial return, it seems to make sense to encourage everyone to attend college. But as we evaluate the real-world outcomes of such a policy, it is evident it is not the appropriate choice for every individual. If we disaggregate the data, it is a far more complicated picture.

First, many individuals made bigger bets on college than they could reasonably afford, and their quality of life has suffered as a result. Our current borrowing mess partly stems from the mentality that the pursuit of college is valuable at *any* cost.

This group includes individuals like Kate Brotherton of Cincinnati, who wrote an op-ed in September 2012 exposing the financial and emotional chaos over having $188,307.22 in student debt from a BA and an MA. "My future and dreams are six feet under, and I am still digging my grave," she wrote.[1] Does anyone believe that Kate's long-term financial prospects ("I still sleep in my parents' basement and am dependent for food, gas and health insurance") are as lucrative as someone who may be without a four-year college degree but has a decent job and an appreciable amount of determination to succeed?

Secondly, the BA-for-all view assumes that a student always finishes what he starts. Yet according to the US Department of Education, only 58 percent of all first-time college students who started at four-year schools in 2004 graduated within six years.[2] Beyond that time frame, it becomes increasingly unlikely that students will have graduated at all.

Those who are quick to urge everyone to get a BA assume that everyone who enrolls in a four-year degree program finishes one. This is far from the case. Why should America tell its high school graduates that college is always the best investment, when many pay an enormous amount of money for no degree?

What should people who are eager to put everyone in a four-year BA program tell this woman from Massachusetts who was featured in a *Washington Post* story?

> Malainie Smith spent a year at a small liberal-arts college in Massachusetts before deciding to go to nursing school. She was halfway through her program at Simmons College in Boston when she took what she thought would be a break of one semester. When she tried to return, she found she could no longer get a loan.
>
> Smith said that left her in a Catch-22 situation. She had to quit school but still owed about $100,000 to the Vermont Student Assistance Corp. (VSAC), a public nonprofit student lender. Her monthly payments are about $400. Three years after she left Simmons, she is now a waitress—a recent promotion from her position as a hostess.[3]

Malainie Smith is a living example of the error of encouraging everyone to get a BA.

Third, as we have discussed previously, data indicate the high return on investment for a BA largely depends on the subject studied and the school attended. This inflates the averages for what the average college graduate's lifetime earnings will be. An international relations major from a subpar school will have a much more difficult time attaining gainful employment in her career field than a chemistry major from Duke. Moreover, bachelor's degree holders often choose later to attend graduate school, an investment that also historically leads to higher wages. When extremely lucrative professions that require a BA, like doctor, lawyer, and investment banker, are taken out of the equation, the *average* earnings from a college degree dip.

Fourth, with the unemployment rate for recent graduates hovering around 50 percent, we suspect the calculus for the return on college is likely to change. Historically, the ROI from purchasing a college degree has stayed fairly consistent. But (and we are not at all happy at this prospect) with a glut of BA holders either unemployed or forced to take part-time positions, often unrelated to their fields of study, it becomes clear that the investment in college, for many, has already depreciated in value.

Fifth, proponents of the college-for-all mentality often assume that people who do not attend college will otherwise make poor choices in life, vocationally or otherwise. In reality, there are a host of other choices—attending community college, acquiring vocational training, enlisting in the military, or starting your own business—that can bring the same (or greater) ROI as college. Moreover, as we have seen previously, a college degree is not absolutely necessary for a satisfying life. People without college degrees get married, start families, find fulfilling work, and often garner a unique satisfaction in taking nontraditional life paths. In the end, character traits and intelligence are more important than any piece of sheepskin.

Last, even if every single American worker had a degree from a four-year college, there would still be workers earning low incomes. A college degree alone cannot mitigate all of the vicissitudes of human existence—poor performance in the workplace, illness, financial mismanagement, a bad economy, and so on. To put it another way, let's say a Democrat from California moves to Texas, a traditionally Republican state. Just having residency in the state of Texas doesn't automatically change that individual's political views, just as a college degree will not automatically equate to high earnings. Many college-for-all theorists think that merely having a diploma will produce higher wages. But it fails to account for a principle of specialization that is required for a thriving economy.

Christopher Caldwell addressed the flawed reasoning of college-for-all enthusiasts in the *Claremont Review of Books* with a football analogy:

> High education is correlated with high incomes in this country, true, but the correlation is based on relative education levels, not absolute ones. Those (our president included) who believe that everyone can receive today's college-level salaries if everyone can be sent to college do not understand how specialization works. They might as well argue that, because kickers score more points than offensive linemen, the best NFL team would have 53 kickers on it.[4]

Direction at the K–12 Level

The move away from this BA-for-all philosophy and mentality must begin at the K–12 level. First, there must be an honest approach by parents, teachers, and guidance counselors to help make students considering college aware of their ability, talents, and inclinations for different types of work other than what they might hope to obtain with a bachelor's degree. Students should be presented with honest, challenging data to help them make the best decisions. For instance, among college freshmen who graduated in the bottom 40 percent of their high school class, seventy-six of one hundred won't earn a diploma, even if given eight and a half years.[5] Likewise, one study found that two-thirds of college students in Kentucky and Ohio requiring remedial course work at four-year colleges failed to earn a degree within six years.[6]

Faced with this data, who would not consider it his professional responsibility to encourage an average or below-average student at least to consider more options other than a four-year college? Before this high school graduate gets slapped with $20,000 of debt to attend a subpar college from which he is unlikely to graduate, he should be presented with statistics like these. He should have as much awareness as possible about the statistical likelihood of his plan succeeding. He should be told that there is no shame in not having a college degree—just ask Steve Jobs, Ted Turner, Rachael Ray, Wally "Famous" Amos, Oracle CEO Larry Ellison, and Whole Food's cofounder John Mackey.[7] He should be given diagnostic tests and honest counsel to help him determine what other educational paths, like community college or trade school, are viable options.

Redirecting the K–12 Curricula

More importantly, however, he needs confidence that the K–12 system has equipped him for the workforce. At the beginning of his first term, President Barack Obama called for every American to commit to at least one year of postsecondary education. His heart may be in the right place—he wants to see American workers compete in the global economy. And the correlation between having only a high school diploma and making less money than college graduates is clear. But President Obama should have also been calling for increased responsibility for the K–12 system to teach students real skills that will be useful to them for securing productive, long-term careers.

Andy Kessler, a research analyst, hedge fund manager, and venture capitalist, recently took to the pages of the *Weekly Standard* to call for a reorientation of the nation's K–12 curriculum with the skills that will be needed in the future. Taking the sciences as but one example, Kessler wrote,

> Biology is important, but too many high school curricula revolve around designing waste management plants and the biodiversity of rain forests. Even Darwin has been marginalized to less than a week. We need to get back to basics and add more genomics and DNA sequencing. Chemistry and physics are important disciplines. I've been told that any science with an adjective attached to its name is probably not a real science, but we should add useful tools for the mass of graduates that end up in sales and marketing. Behavioral science, psychology, organization science, decision theory, and, of course, statistics. Everybody hates statistics,

> thinking it the language of dull actuaries. But statistics and data are the core ingredients to how Facebook pages are arranged and Google search results are displayed and every web page looks and operates. No one guesses anymore.[8]

A reorientation of curriculum with employer demand doesn't just mean shoving as many students as possible into physics classes. This also means providing vocational education that will allow students to obtain decent-paying jobs right after graduation—skills that will benefit a law firm, a hospital, a mechanic's shop, or an airline.

In light of the country's growing need for skilled labor jobs, both now and in the future, K–12 institutions should be especially committed to reinstituting the sort of vocational education that has slowly disappeared over the past few decades. We mean things like plumbing, welding, electrical work, and machine shop skills.

There is a great misconception among students, parents, and the educational establishment that if you do this kind of work for a career, your mind is second rate and not up to a desirable par. On the contrary, much of the work in these fields today requires a highly detailed skill set and a familiarity with technology that many office workers cannot claim to have. As the writer Matthew Crawford makes clear in his essay "The Case for Working with Your Hands," fixing a motorcycle engine is a complicated process that requires a strong knowledge base and significant ability to reason and think critically. More particularly, these hands-on jobs frequently appeal to boys. Amidst a slow degeneration of the

American man's embrace of work (one in five working-age males in America does not work, down from one in twenty in 1960),[9] these programs can instill a sense of success and purpose to boys who may not be finding it elsewhere, and who may feel alienated from school due to lack of interest or ability at traditional academic work.

In 2008, Mayor Michael Bloomberg of New York announced some new initiatives for promoting vocational education in the New York City school system. "College isn't for everyone, but education is," he said. Bloomberg's statement was confirmed by the "Pathways to Prosperity" report issued by Harvard University in February 2011, which argues that the focus on getting everybody into college actually encourages individuals who perceive the work as too difficult to drop out of high school, thus negating the intended effect of the college prep curriculum. As the report stated, "A narrowly defined 'college for all' goal—one that does not include a much stronger focus on career-oriented programs that lead to occupational credentials—seems doomed to fail."[10]

Apprenticeship Programs, Hybrids, and Trade Schools

One of the key educational institutions that should be revived is the apprenticeship program. Currently, only 0.3 percent of American workers are in some type of apprenticeship program—a hybrid of classroom and hands-on learning that appeals to individuals of different learning styles.[11]

The most prominent criticism of encouraging "hands-on work" is that the global economy has gradually become a service economy, in which traditional blue-collar jobs are in less demand. But making a career out of a job like being an oil and gas field technician shouldn't be considered a pipe dream. Hundreds of thousands of skilled labor jobs currently remain unfilled in the United States, with the gap only expected to grow wider because of baby boomer retirement. Outside the United States, a survey done by the powerhouse consulting firm McKinsey and Company predicted that there would be as many as eighty-five million unfilled skilled labor jobs worldwide by 2020.[12] We are not urging workers to take up low-skill, low-wage blue-collar jobs that require no training and have continually shrunk as a percentage of the economy since the 1970s. We want more individuals to consider the kind of hands-on, *skilled* jobs that employers say they need *right now and for the future.*

Hybrid vocational education, on a smaller scale, would also enrich the students who are in every way qualified for college. As Charles Murray has written, too often "upper-middle-class children can graduate from high school isolated from any contact with a world in which people make their livings by working their hands and without ever knowing the satisfactions that can come from non-academic forms of excellence."[13] On my (Bill's) radio show *Morning in America*, Kansas governor Sam Brownback speculated, "Imagine what kinds of people this country would have if they learned plumbing and went to Harvard."

For those who have graduated from high school and are now considering trade school, we stress the importance of evaluating the school you are considering. Many are diploma mills that do not teach the necessary skills that employers desire. Students must ensure that they will be actually learning things in class, not just hanging out. They need to ensure that the school is accredited by an accrediting agency. If they plan to eventually pursue a bachelor's degree, they should ensure their credits will transfer. They should try to track down some graduates (or dropouts) of the school and see what their experiences were like.

The Military Option

The military is another option for people who want additional career training but do not consider themselves ready or inclined to attend college.

To be clear, the chief aim of military service is serving the nation. But for generations of Americans, the military has been a conduit for acquiring knowledge in technical and nontechnical fields such as computer technology, automotive mechanics, aircraft maintenance, foreign languages, logistics, and communications. The military is also attractive because it sponsors a number of programs that will either help pay for college or repay student loans. This makes sense for those who one day desire to go to college but do not feel prepared just yet. The military is often an excellent and honorable option.

Considerations for Those Going to College

If you have determined to attend college, here are several important considerations:

1. Examine the Data

When you are considering what college to attend, examine with a critical eye as much data as possible, especially related to your finances. PayScale.com has compiled a useful chart of data on colleges, with categories like thirty-year return on investment, average financial aid, and the four-year net cost. Dig deep, and ask the school's financial aid office what the average graduate's indebtedness is upon graduation. Many schools offer financial aid to freshmen and then withdraw it in subsequent years. If the school offers you non-loan financial aid, ask about the likelihood of being offered the same amount each year. The Department of Education has a searchable database of student-loan default rates at each school—check schools at which students are defaulting.

Ignore seductive nonsense that schools pitch, such as glossy brochures of a sunlit campus that urge you to consider whether a school is a "good fit" or will help you "reach your dreams." You are purchasing an expensive product, so you need some measure of confidence in your gut that you are making the right choice. But don't let your impulses of how nice the campus looks or how happy the students appear outweigh the dollars-and-cents calculation of the cost to attend a school.

Senators Marco Rubio and Ron Wyden are realizing the importance of data to parents and students in evaluating higher education choices. That's why they have introduced the Know Before You Go Act in the Senate. Under the proposed bill, the federal government will help states coordinate student educational and postgraduate employment data. The bill's great aim is to help consumers make better choices about the products they are considering. Said Rubio, "We want people to know what the new jobs, skills, careers in the twenty-first century are. The reason you need to know what your professional prospects are is that you have to weigh that against how much you will borrow." He continued, "Including law school, I graduated with $125,000 in student loans. That's nobody's fault—it was an investment for me. We want kids to have access to information before they make this investment."[14]

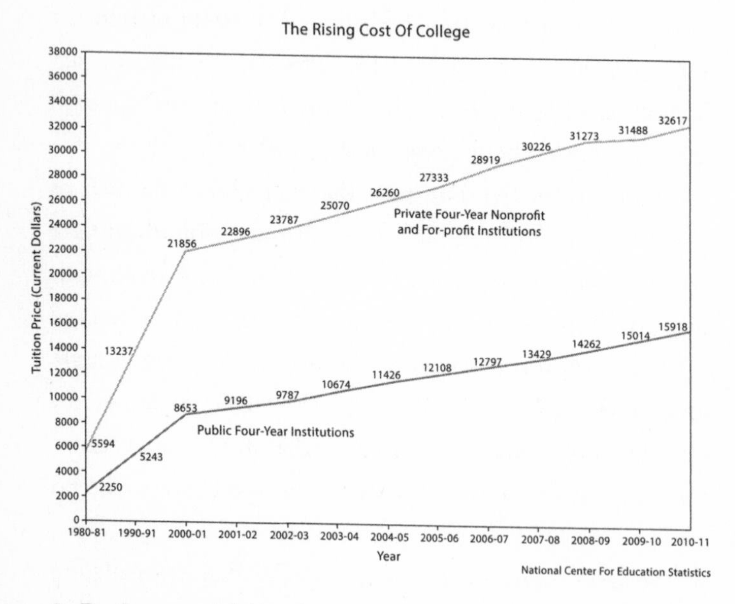

2. Be Smart with Loans

It is of the utmost importance to be as thoughtful as possible in considering taking on debt to pay for college. To start, pay as much as you and your family can afford upfront; loans should be a last resort in paying for school.

Many students borrow money without knowing how much they are borrowing or how much it will cost to pay back the amount. *Never, never, never do this*. Know the details of your loan transaction. Remember that this is real money that will one day come out of your bank account every month. Do not be irrationally optimistic that student-loan debt will simply take care of itself. If you must borrow, the federal government will usually charge you a lower interest rate (learn what that is if you do not know) than private banks and will afford you more leeway in missing payments if you cannot pay.

If you must spend multiple tens of thousands of dollars for a bachelor's degree with no hope of scholarship, non-loan financial aid, or family contributions, odds are you will have difficulty paying back your loans out of college. Reevaluate other educational options that may not seem as attractive in the short term but will benefit you financially in the long run. This might entail going to a less-heralded school or living at home instead of on campus.

Some instructive examples of being smart about paying for college appeared in an article in the *Wall Street Journal*. One student who was accepted to Cornell (price tag: more than $40,000 per year for out-of-state residents) and hopes to one day attend medical school instead decided to attend the Macaulay Honors program at the City University of New York (a new free-tuition undergraduate program for qualifying undergraduates). His rationale? It wasn't "worth it to spend $50,000-plus a year for a bachelor's degree."[15]

This sort of thinking is actually becoming a trend, even among families with more financial resources to pay for school. Sallie Mae released a report in 2011 that showed "twenty-two percent of students from families with annual household incomes above $100,000 attended public, two-year schools in the 2010–2011 academic year, up from 12 percent the previous year."[16] In brief, even rich kids are choosing community college, often hoping to excel there and then transfer to a four-year state school to finish a BA.

Especially if you think you may want to attend graduate school one day, which will entail further expenditures, it may not even be worth it to immediately attend an expensive school, even if it is elite. You can distinguish yourself to graduate schools through excellent grades and standardized test scores, even if you do not attend one of the best of the best schools in the country. Harvard Law School, for instance, featured students from 161 institutions for the 2012–13 school year, including ones from relatively unknown schools like Hendrix College, Walla Walla College, and the University of Northern Iowa.[17]

And if you needed any more confirmation that attending an elite school is no guarantee of a large paycheck, may we remind you that PaysScale.com data indicated the average 2012 graduate of the South Dakota School of Mines & Technology earned more than the average graduate of Harvard University in that year? With the US economy in dire need of skilled workers in the commodities extraction industry, the earnings premium for entering a high-demand field outweighs the benefits of having a degree from the most prestigious school in the world. "It doesn't seem to be too hard to get a job in mining," said Jaymie Trask, a twenty-two-year-old chemical engineering major who was offered a post paying more than $60,000 a year at Copper & Gold Inc. "If you work hard in school for four or five years, you're pretty much set."[18]

3. Get a Good Education

Amidst all the talk about the financial return of a college degree, remember that you will actually have to choose what you will learn, and learning is the chief purpose of attending college. We've already shown that STEM (science, technology, engineering, and mathematics) graduates have a greater probability of getting hired and, on average, have higher starting salaries than those for social science or humanities disciplines. But the classical liberal arts (history, literature, classics, philosophy, and religion), if properly taught and studied, will equip a student to know the best that Western civilization has to offer, and these studies can be—and are—extremely intellectually rewarding. There is a reason that many core works have been taught for centuries: their value is inherent to those who read them. Knowing these works allows us to understand our nation and civilization. But if you do major in liberal arts or a social science (psychology, sociology, political science), understand that your employment prospects, especially in the current economy, may be limited, even dramatically so.

Some students may desire to become familiar with the classics of Western civilization but do not deem it so valuable as to be worth the high price of a college education, especially with limited employment prospects. Yet new ways of engaging with these classic texts are emerging. One such method is a company called Great Courses, which offers audio and video lectures by top professors on subjects from ancient philosophy to calculus to cocktail mixing for students to watch or listen to whenever they like. Reflecting the high demand for such classic (and practical) content, business is booming at Great Courses. *Forbes* reported that after a rough first few years, Great Courses is now selling $110 million worth of material each year.[19] Sadly, this is material that students sometimes cannot find on their own campuses. So they turn to the commercial market to get, as Matthew Arnold said, "the best which has been thought and said."

If you want to learn about the Western or other traditions in a more social setting, a model set up by a group calling itself the Brooklyn Institute for Social Research has a novel approach. Hoping to help out impecunious graduate students while fulfilling the public's desire to explore the Western canon, the Brooklyn Institute meets in a back room in a bar in Brooklyn once a week and charges each student $295 per course, which lasts about six weeks. In exchange, a lecturer, usually a PhD student, teaches something connected to the Western intellectual tradition. Last spring, for example, a Columbia University doctoral student taught a high-level class on Plato and Aristotle to a group of students.

"I do really, really want to reach out to people who maybe never had a college opportunity at all," founder and instructor Ajay Singh Chaudhary said. "No, you do not have to have a college degree to come study here. But we are not dumbing anything down. We think it's possible to teach this to a very diverse group."[20]

4. Set Your Expectations Appropriately

Last, manage your expectations for what you can expect to obtain from your college education. If you devote yourself to getting top grades in a high-demand field, you will have a much better chance of landing a job upon graduation. However, *a college degree doesn't guarantee you a job.* Conversely, if hypothetically you accept a great deal of debt to major in a subject for which employers are expressing little demand, understand that there is a very high probability of high student-loan payments without adequate salary to cover them.

This was one of the chief grievances of the Occupy Wall Street movement—many of the demonstrators were upset at having a college degree that they believed to be useless, insofar as they were unemployed or underemployed. Their expectation that college equals financial success led to a great deal of misplaced anger.

SPECIFIC SCHOOLS

No school is uniformly perfect, and there is no math equation for determining exactly where a student should go to college, but several schools and kinds of schools have stood out to us for different reasons. Some are quite out of the mainstream, idiosyncratic, and nevertheless very worthy. These schools fall outside our previously recommended schools in chapter 3. As we discussed in that chapter, based on returns on investment and other factors, if a student gets into an Ivy League school, that student should probably go. Furthermore, if a student is accepted into an elite institution like the University of Chicago or Harvey Mudd College, usually that student should go. The average lifetime earnings of graduates of this caliber of schools far exceed the tuition costs.

But recognizing that the vast majority of college students will not be admitted to these institutions, we want to point out a group of fairly selective public universities with friendly in-state tuition prices and above-average academic reputations. We detailed many of these in chapter 3 too. They include the University of North Carolina, the University of Texas, the University of Michigan, and the University of Virginia. William and Mary College in Virginia also has a sterling academic reputation at a reasonable in-state and out-of-state cost ($13,000 and $25,000, respectively). These schools have enough name recognition to make their graduates favorable to employers. But before you decide to choose a major at these or any other schools, make sure that there is enough substantive content taught in class. If you are a philosophy major, for instance, make sure you will be studying great thinkers like Plato or Locke, not the rapper Jay-Z (on whom Georgetown University has offered a class).[21]

Outside these schools we get to our aforementioned unique schools that caught our attention. First, there is a growing cohort of schools grounded in the traditions of the liberal arts and the Christian faith that will appeal to many readers of this book. These schools offer a classroom environment of meaty academics and a campus social culture far removed from the typical dorm experience in America today.

Patrick Henry College, in Purcellville, Virginia, is a small, selective, evangelical school, often dubbed "The Harvard of the Homeschooled," about an hour from Washington, DC. Its proximity to the city affords students numerous opportunities to involve themselves in the nation's political life. Moreover, Patrick Henry's tuition is only about $24,000 a year, a good value in the current marketplace. Similarly, Grove City College in Grove City, Pennsylvania, is another bargain school with strong academics and an evangelical worldview. Charging only around $21,000 per year, Grove City has been stoutly committed to the liberal arts tradition since 1876.

For those who are more adventurous, New Saint Andrews College in Moscow, Idaho, is a tiny Reformed evangelical school that has modeled its course offerings on the curriculum that Harvard employed in 1643. This includes incorporating the ancient approach to learning of the trivium (grammar, rhetoric, and dialectic) and the quadrivium (arithmetic, geometry, astronomy, and music). While new student enrollment is limited to fifty students each year, the academics are rigorous, and the small size of the college ensures that the faculty and staff of the college bond in uncommonly deep ways with students, including spiritual ones. Additionally, NSA's tuition is only $16,000 per year, about one-third the cost of the average private college.

There are similar schools in the Catholic tradition. The University of Dallas (2,700 students) and Thomas Aquinas College (359 students) in Santa Paula, California, are two small schools committed to traditional Catholic doctrines of spirituality, while teaching a liberal arts curriculum of Western civilization. Both charge tuitions far below the national average. The Catholic University of America, in Washington, DC, has also preserved a Catholic approach to the liberal arts and is moving in a more traditional direction in terms of student life—last year it began to convert all of its dorms, formerly mixed in gender, to single-sex residences. CUA's tuition prices, however, are in line with the national averages.

One of the newest, but also most promising, institutions in the same vein is Wyoming Catholic College. Founded in 2005, Wyoming Catholic is a four-year private Catholic institution committed to a liberal arts education. In fact, it offers an integrated Great Books curriculum and only grants students a BA in liberal arts. This ensures that all graduates are well prepared for life and the workforce with a deep, grounded education and the ability to think critically. Saint Katherine College is a nascent liberal arts and sciences school outside San Diego, California, religiously affiliated with the Eastern Orthodox tradition. It offers BA and science degrees in art, biological sciences, biotechnology, chemistry and biochemistry, economics, English language and literature, history, management science, music, philosophy, public policy, and theology. The school's motto, "Inquiry Seeking Wisdom," captures the school's broad commitment not only to a traditional teaching of the liberal arts but also a special focus on the sciences, an area of study that is often underemphasized at Christian colleges. Saint Katherine College modestly sets its tuition at $17,500 per year, as of this writing.

For those interested in a classic liberal arts education not of a particular religious affiliation, there is Hillsdale College in Hillsdale, Michigan. Founded in 1844, Hillsdale has long centered its curriculum on the classics of Western heritage and the principles of America's founding. Hillsdale (along with Grove City and Patrick Henry) is one of the few colleges in the nation that does not accept federal funding, meaning it can come under no federal pressure to adapt or modify its curriculum.

We realize that a liberal arts major or small-school environment is not for everyone. Western Governors University (WGU) is an appealing nonprofit online venture that has developed a very promising model. WGU was started in 1995 by several governors in the western United States who felt compelled to address the difficult synergy of shrinking state budgets for higher education and growing populations. WGU was founded shortly thereafter.

Recognizing that most of its students are working adults, WGU focuses on granting BA and MA degrees in only a few core disciplines: business, nursing, IT, and teaching. But instead of advancing and graduating students based on credit hours taken, it focuses on advancing students on their ability to demonstrate competency in a subject. In this way, the university and its students can cut costs and save time. The average for-profit universities charge about $15,600 per year. Tuition at Western Governors costs a flat rate of just under $6,000 a year, for as many courses as the student wants to take. The student can take as much time as he or she needs to work through the material. In addition, all students take preassessment tests that allow them to forgo material they have already mastered. One pastor who was working toward an MBA, for instance, aced his preassessment test in business ethics since he had studied the subject intensively while studying for his BA in ministry and theology.

WGU also develops its curriculum with a view of students acing professional licensure exams. Teachers, for instance, are prepared to do well on the increasingly important Praxis exam required by many states. Perhaps most important, WGU students benefit from professional mentors, who make frequent contact with their students to help them make the best choices for their educational career. This is a unique and crucial feature in an environment where so many students are perhaps entering college for the first time in their thirties or forties. WGU's student loan default rate is only about 5 percent, much lower than the 25 percent average of for-profits. Ultimately, it's no coincidence that the WGU has recently grown at a pace of about 30 percent per year, and that several states, including Indiana and Texas, are partnering with WGU to make it affiliated with their own state university systems.[22]

Generally, we advise that if a student can afford to attend a top private school without amassing outrageous amounts of debt, he or she should go. Sadly, we do not always say this because the learning is always of the top caliber. Rather, degrees from these schools are distinguished and attractive to employers, and you can, in school, build professional networks with individuals who are one day likely to be at the top of their fields. However, even an Ivy League education might not be worth multiple tens of thousands of dollars each year in loans. Carefully consider your current and future financial circumstances, especially if you are majoring in the liberal arts or social sciences. (Recall the student who opted for the Macaulay Honors program at CUNY over Cornell.)

Make sure you are learning something of real value, not endless academic speculation that will never help you do anything on the job. If you are technologically minded, Stanford University gets credit from us for facilitating a culture in which students, faculty, and business leaders from Silicon Valley have an easy exchange of ideas and interactions. This helps students make connections that will help them land jobs after graduation in the lucrative tech hub of Northern California. On the retail dimension of picking a college, it is also one of the most beautiful campuses in America. Likewise, we would recommend without hesitation that a student talented enough to get into a top-tier technical school like Harvey Mudd, MIT, the Colorado School of Mines, or Caltech should go.

We acknowledge that most students aren't going to attend a school as selective as Harvey Mudd or a place with traditional values like Grove City or Patrick Henry. But even if you do not go to a top-tier school or a religiously orthodox school, you can still get a quality education. If you find yourself at a school that is, by various measures, academically subpar, don't fret that you've somehow failed at life. Continue to surround yourself with like-minded people, who will sharpen, not stifle, your best qualities. Find individuals who share your faith or politics and are studying the same subjects you are. Socially, much of the value of college comes from studying complex topics and walking through life with your peers. Don't neglect these experiences, no matter where you go.

Additionally (and this may take some work), find a professor or two who shares your passions for a subject or your values. There are still many professors who enjoy meeting with and teaching like-minded students. They can usually help you navigate adverse personal circumstances and offer professional guidance.

Last, expand your knowledge outside class, and apply it in a way that will be enriching to you and impressive to employers. Take internships, write for the school newspaper, attend panel discussions, or volunteer. You will likely never have more free time in your life than you will during college. Maximize your opportunities now before the obligations of a full-time job and family compel you to make sacrifices of your time, money, and energy.

For the Very Gifted

For the individuals who are so intellectually gifted that spending four years in college may actually be a hindrance to developing their potential, new programs are sprouting up that encourage a flourishing of intellectual gifts outside the traditional college experience. The goal of these programs is that, in lieu of college, students will obtain the connections and capital they need to make waves in fields like business, technology, and learning.

As we previously mentioned, one such program has been

started by Peter Thiel, the billionaire cofounder of PayPal and one of the most vocal critics of higher education, who believes that college classrooms are doing little to equip our future CEOs, innovators, and industry leaders. Thiel has a point. Some of the brightest students might be better off not going to college at all, being forced to take classes in which they have no interest and leaving with burdensome student-loan debt. Addressing this reality, Thiel took things into his own hands and started the 20 Under 20 Thiel Fellowship, a program that brings together the most enterprising students younger than twenty and offers them a $100,000 grant to skip college and explore their own research and entrepreneurial ideas. Under the tutelage of investors, scientists, and like-minded industry tycoons, students are able to develop connections, court investors, and promote their businesses on a level that Thiel says colleges cannot provide. According to James O'Neill, head of the Thiel Foundation, more than ten of the fellows have started their own companies, and one of them released his own product on the market.

Another, similar program is the the E[nstitute] in New York. Founded by a twenty-five-year-old and a thirty-year-old, the E[nstitute] was specifically designed to train students gifted in entrepreneurship. Students must be between eighteen and twenty-four and commit to the two-year program, which costs $60,000. Many of the students previously attended college and realized that it was not the best avenue for nurturing their talents. At the E[nstitute], students work directly with the founders of some of the most dynamic start-up companies in New York—the lifestyle website Thrillist and eyewear designer Warby Parker, to name just two.[23] Like the Thiel Fellowship, this model is attractive to students with a gift for business who feel comfortable forgoing college. But it could also presage a larger trend in higher education, wherein schools recognize students' specialties and pair them directly with firms that will give them the relevant hands-on training. For many, doing this would save time and money while offering valuable workplace experience.

Character and Personal Attributes Matter the Most

Students have many options to pursue after high school. But whether a student enters the workforce out of high school, attends college, or obtains a Thiel Fellowship, personal attributes like discipline, self-control, perseverance, and communication skills matter more for ultimate personal and financial success than what any piece of paper says about you. College may signal to employers a certain level of achievement or just perseverance, but in the long run, that will matter little if you can't demonstrate honesty, commitment, and a willingness to be held accountable for your actions. In other words, intangible character traits still supersede other environmental factors.

The writer Paul Tough recently demonstrated this in his new book *How Children Succeed*, which explored a new wave of data from around the scientific spectrum that emphasizes the importance of character traits to life achievement. One of the people Tough studied was a teenager from an impoverished neighborhood in Chicago who did not strike Tough as being particularly intelligent. Nor did she have any of the social advantages that are often characteristic of high-achieving students. Yet, according to Tough, "What was most remarkable to me about Kewauna was that she was able to marshal her prodigious noncognitive capacity—call it grit, conscientiousness, resilience, or the ability to delay gratification—all for a distant prize that was, for her, almost entirely theoretical."[24] Today, Kewauna is thriving in college.

According to Tough, this emphasis on character also explains the success of children at the KIPP Academy, a network of K-12 charter schools for underprivileged students that sets extremely high standards for its students:

> [T]here is this way that certain high-pressure academic environments can stress kids out. They are on this treadmill versus climbing a mountain. At KIPP kids are climbing a mountain and it's a bigger challenge than staying on that familiar treadmill. I think that's why KIPP kids get out of college with more success and character. It's the way you get on a life path, not the actual life path you end up on, and that makes all the difference.[25]

Things Colleges Are Doing To Reform

Peter Thiel's fellowship represents a philosophy that has the potential to disrupt America's current approach to higher education. Thiel's fellowship is proof of his belief that Americans have invested too much—literally and figuratively—in the value of a college degree. In order for higher education to remain a product that the public wants to purchase, it may have to apply some Thiel-style thinking to its own models. We do not mean that every college should shutter its doors, but these schools may have to institute some challenging reforms in order to avoid massive budget gaps or intellectual irrelevance. We have already suggested reforms like having greater accountability at all levels, teaching meaningful materials, and stewarding resources in a more responsible manner. But there is still potential for unusual solutions to the weighty problems facing the educational establishment. These reforms may be institutionally uncomfortable, but they are necessary for the sake of students and schools alike.

In 2011, Texas governor Rick Perry challenged schools in his state to offer a bachelor's degree for the total cost of $10,000. The University of Texas–Arlington responded to the call, and in partnership with the Mansfield, Texas, school district, is offering just that. Students in the Mansfield school district will be eligible to earn twenty-four hours of college credits in their junior and senior years and then take them to Tarrant County College to earn an associate's degree in two years. Upon completion of course work, they can then transfer to UT–Arlington for a bachelor's degree in two years. The students are not allowed to drop out or take a break in their course of studies, and they must be selected for the program. In exchange for working hard over the course of the sequence, they are eligible for special tuition breaks and financial aid that could save each student $25,000 off the sticker price of their baccalaureate degree.

"There's a real demand for higher education, and at the same time lawmakers have been calling for efficiencies," said Kristin Sullivan, assistant vice president for media relations at UT–Arlington. "This is aligning courses at the high school level with community colleges and with the four-year level, to make sure the courses count," Sullivan told the *Ft. Worth Star-Telegram*.[26]

At the University of Texas at Permian Basin, students with a 3.0 GPA majoring in geology, chemistry, computer science, information systems, or math, can also attend for $10,000. The $10,000 degree program is also being developed at eight other colleges in the UT system. This kind of reform—one that links students' decisions to major in competitive disciplines with a reduced tuition—is a serious step in addressing both the crippling cost of college and America's skills shortage.

Schools should also make data plentifully available to students so that they can complete their degrees in a timely and efficient manner. More than eight hundred colleges and universities have already partnered with a company called MyEdu, which, among its other functions, disaggregates data on professors, grades, and classes at partner schools, so that students may make smarter choices when planning their academic courses, hence increasing their likelihood of graduating on time. MyEdu is also about to start partnering with employers searching for competitive graduates. Employers will post on the MyEdu jobs page the specific skills they are looking for in potential hires, and the hope is that students will tailor their academic careers to meet those demands.

Stanford University, one of the best schools in the country, has unofficially adopted a business-friendly institutional philosophy that brings together students, faculty, and employers in formal and informal settings. One professor of entrepreneurship and venture capital, himself the founder of a venture capital firm, invites sixteen venture capitalists a year to his class. This allows for a fluid exchange of ideas and information, and for employers to get to know students individually. Consequently, it is not a coincidence that a great percentage of Silicon Valley's brainpower comes from Stanford. Of course, these students are already gifted in their field, but the access that Stanford provides for top talent to communicate with one another gives students a distinct advantage of a personal relationship with a potential employer.

Educational establishments should make it their mission to link students with employers in their fields. Often, the academic establishment is suspicious of business interests, thinking that their influence will stifle free expression of academic views. To the contrary, programs in business, the sciences, and other practical disciplines should promote close contact with businesses that might be interested in teaching them something on their visit and hiring their graduates.

Another reform at Stanford is under way in the liberal arts. Professor Russell Berman and five others have called for a revision of how universities approach graduate studies in the liberal arts. Realizing that too many students take nearly a decade of study to complete a PhD in the humanities, a credential that leaves them ill prepared for the job market, Stanford professors have declared, "The study of the humanities needs to be accessible and cheap. And we need to be more transparent about our placement records."[27]

Consequently, Berman and his colleagues are calling for a four- or five-year PhD program that would grant funding to students during the summertime to expedite the process. Additionally, they have realized that graduate programs in the liberal arts do too little to prepare students for nonacademic career options. Graduate programs, they wrote, "should aim to balance academic training in a particular discipline and field with the provision of broader professional perspectives that may extend beyond the traditional academic setting." The University of Colorado's PhD program in German studies has already moved in this direction, with the University of Minnesota's graduate school looking into doing the same.[28] We encourage reforms in graduate programs in the humanities that will hasten graduation and eschew debt.

ONLINE EDUCATION IS BOOMING

One of the greatest hopes for reforming higher education lies in digital learning. The concept is not entirely new—the University of Phoenix offered its first online degree in 1989,[29] and more than one million students, many of them nontraditional students working full-time, take a class online every year. Over the last few years, however, the higher education community has embraced new online ventures in ways they never have before, with many anticipating that it will one day become the norm for college learning. Colleges and investors are putting their money where their mouth is. Investments in education-technology companies totaled $429 million in 2011, according to the National Venture Capital Association. That's compared to only $146 million in 2002.[30]

Some of the most prestigious schools in America are already embracing the new percolations, offering several free courses to the public over the Internet. In May 2012, Harvard and MIT teamed up and invested $60 million combined funds in edX, an online learning venture that allowed for open access to STEM material. At the news conference announcing the venture, officials described the potential of online learning as "the single biggest change in education since the printing press."[31] UC–Berkeley became a partner in the venture the following July.

In 2012, several members of the University of Virginia's Board of Visitors tried to force out the University of Virginia's president, Teresa Sullivan. In the ensuing controversy, an e-mail surfaced from a Board of Visitors member who supported Sullivan's involuntary dismissal. The writer of the e-mail made clear Sullivan was to be removed largely because the board felt Sullivan was not properly embracing the changing landscape of the university classroom. "The decision of the Board of Visitors to move in another direction stems from their concern that the governance of the University was not sufficiently tuned to the dramatic changes we all face: funding, Internet, technology advances, the new economic model,"[32] he wrote.

David Brooks, a conservative columnist at the *New York Times*, has made an analogy of the digitalization of higher education to that of the newspaper industry: "What happened to the newspaper and magazine business is about to happen to higher education: a rescrambling around the Web."[33] John Hennessy, the president of Stanford University, put it even more succinctly: "There's a tsunami coming."[34] It is clear that many gatekeepers in the higher education community believe in the power of online learning to reshape the entire structure of higher ed.

MASSIVE OPEN ONLINE COURSES

In higher education, the prime driver of the growing ed-tech phenomenon is the high potential for online courses to increase access to educational content while lowering the costs. If one professor can teach a few hundred students in a lecture hall, why can't one professor teach thousands of students online in multiple sections of the same course? More and more institutions are putting this idea into practice in courses called MOOCs—massive open online courses.

There are many advantages to the MOOC model. Hundreds or thousands of individuals, many who are members of the general public unaffiliated with the school, can enroll in a course. The lectures and reading assignments are often downloaded from a common Web page and can be accessed any time. For students (particularly working adults), this is a wonderful prospect. Why be forced to show up for a 2:00 p.m. brick-and-mortar class when you could take it online at 6:00 a.m., before work, with prerecorded video lectures? Tests, quizzes, and homework can be handed in online. If students don't understand the material, they can caucus together on message boards and e-mail chains to help one another and give ratings to the most helpful responses to a topic discussed in class. Schools can save money by spending money on an extraordinary professor who teaches one lesson instead of six average professors who teach the same subject in a physical classroom. New lecture halls do not have to be built, with floors to sweep and rooms to be heated. More important, with many nonmatriculating students enrolling in these classes, schools fulfill their stated mission of being educators.

One of the men responsible for what may be an Athens-like renaissance in higher education is Sebastian Thrun, Google's vice president and pioneer in artificial intelligence and robotics. Known in science circles for his engineering feats—like Stanley, the self-driving car—Thrun is using his technological prowess to make quality higher education available to the world.

In 2011, while teaching a graduate-level artificial intelligence class at Stanford University, Thrun lamented that his course could reach only two hundred students in the suburbs of Palo Alto. So, he decided to offer his own free online class, with the same homework, quizzes, and tests that he gives to Stanford students. He announced the proposal with a single e-mail. Before he knew it, he had a flood of takers. I (Bill) asked him about it on *Morning in America*. "Usually I reach about 200 students and now I reach 160,000," said Thrun incredulously. "In my entire life of education I didn't have as much an impact on people as I had in these two months."

By using online videos and educational resources, Thrun's class was being accessed by students from all corners of the world. In fact, the students translated the class for free from English into forty-four languages.

Until now, an overwhelming number of these students—many in developing countries and lacking standard education credentials—never would have had a chance at a Stanford-level education. Yet their appetite for quality education was strong. When Thrun began testing his new hoard of students, of all the students taking his class globally and at Stanford, the top 410 students were online students. The 411th top performer was a Stanford student. "We just found over 400 people in the world who outperformed the top Stanford student," Thrun said.

Realizing the potential at his fingertips, Thrun launched Udacity, an independent online education company that provides high-quality education at low cost to virtually everyone.[35] It also offers eleven STEM courses, like Introduction to Physics, Intro to Computer Science, and Web Application Engineering—all free. There are no admissions offices, and anyone can sign up. After the class, students can choose to certify their skills online or in one of Udacity's 4,500 testing centers for a fee. Those certificates can then be sent to employers. In one course you can learn to make your own Google-style search engine in just seven weeks.

The reaction has been overwhelming. "People really

want good education. There is a huge need," Thrun said. "Hundreds of thousands of people just sign up because they really care. They really want to advance themselves and their lives, and they don't want to pay $50,000 or $100,000 to get there."

The classes are structured much like university classes. But instead of traditional types of lectures, all-star professors give video presentations that directly engage and challenge students. Thrun is using technology not only to transform educational access and curricula but also teaching. For the past thousand years, professors have been lecturing at students. "[It's] like trying to lose weight by watching a professor exercise," quips Thrun. Now he is leading a new charge—interactive, student-focused technology education.

The results are inspiring. On *Morning in America* early one morning, several listeners called in to say they already took classes through Udacity. One man had his sights set on graduate school but was too busy with family and work to ever finish along a traditional path. Now, through Udacity, he can take the STEM classes he wants when he wants. Another man, age fifty-three, decided to change careers and go back to a local college to study computer science. When he heard of Udacity, he dropped out of school and signed up for an online course. He said he learned more in several weeks with Udacity than he did in an entire semester at the local college, and he paid nothing for it.

As you can imagine, Thrun's enterprise has rattled the foundations of the education establishment. His critics say that a Udacity certificate is worth nothing, and how can one know the true identity or scholastic work of a student on the free-for-all jungle that is the Internet?

We raised these questions to Thrun. He said Udacity has already partnered with more than twenty companies that verify and accept the certificates of course completion. Some are already hiring graduates of Udacity courses. Thrun is also working with other companies to design and tailor classes to specific needs in the workforce. Soon, Udacity will be launching in-person testing centers to verify a student's knowledge and skills.

Udacity is simultaneously meeting the educational needs of the public and the vocational requirements of the labor force directly and efficiently, more so than we can say of many universities and colleges. Recently, Udacity formed a partnership with San Jose State University, offering low-level math classes for credit to SJSU students for only $150 per course.

We asked Thrun whether his enterprise and others like it will be the end of higher education as we know it—exclusive enclaves for a limited number of students at high tuitions. "I think it's the beginning of higher education," Thrun replied.

Much of traditional American higher education prides itself on a false promotion of diversity, opportunity, and excellence. But to our knowledge, with one class alone, Thrun has provided a level of diversity, opportunity, and academic rigor not seen before. People from any country, any background, and any income level can receive an elite education at virtually no cost. We have been talking about equal educational opportunity for years. This may be its true advent.

MOOC Disadvantages

But like every educational model, MOOCs are not without their disadvantages. For one thing, an entirely online education does not at present have the same reputation of quality that is associated with brick-and-mortar classrooms. As we have discussed, universities, unlike other businesses, do not always try to increase the supply of their product. The top schools instead depend on a scarcity of product to make it more attractive to consumers. The public has internalized this perception, and hence online education is often regarded as inferior in quality.

The revolution in online education is being driven by the desire to optimize productivity. But education is also a social experience, in which the process and not just the outcome is critical to the student's flourishing. MOOCs have the potential to diminish student-teacher interaction and the Socratic discourse between student and teacher that can be vital to developing a student's thinking and reasoning process.

We are referring here to the pedagogical style that has played a crucial role in the Western intellectual tradition, beginning with the philosopher Socrates himself. In the ideal iteration of the Socratic method, students and teachers explore a topic through intense questioning, pushing one another to question their assumptions and refine their reasoning processes to arrive at conclusions. In a study conducted by Williams College, researchers found that the strongest factor in predicting student success was contact with professors.[36]

To a cynic, this might mean that familiar associations

between student and teacher might indicate an unfair presence of favoritism when grades are awarded. This might be true in some cases, but overall, the data seems to justify the high-value process of mutual inquiry that has played a critical role in Western learning. The preservation of the Socratic method is especially important to the humanities, where expansive questions about religion, philosophy, art, history, and literature have persisted without absolute agreement since mankind started considering them. This is not a rejection of the MOOCs but a challenge, and perhaps MOOCs can respond in part by noting the volume of online interaction they display among their students.

In other disciplines, ones characterized by quantitative analysis such as mathematics, physics, astronomy, or computer science, "concrete" answers are critical to understanding the material and advancing further in the discipline. The value of the Socratic method should not be not diminished here either, but perhaps these fields will prove to be more suitable to be offered online, precisely because a premium is placed at arriving at data-driven answers in these fields. Consequently, many MOOC courses have bet heavily on these types of subjects. In the first round of courses offered by the Harvard–MIT venture edX, STEM courses like Introduction to Solid State Chemistry, Circuits and Electronics, and Artificial Intelligence were exclusively offered. Sebastian Thrun's Udacity made the same choice: courses there are subjects like Differential Equations in Action and Programming Languages.

Another disadvantage of MOOCs is a potential for plagiarism and cheating. When so much homework and testing is done in absolute privacy, students may find it easier to transgress the rules on academic dishonesty. Numerous instances of plagiarism were recently reported in humanities courses offered by Coursera.[37] Since many MOOCs currently do not offer academic credit, it may be easy for anyone trying to attain a credential for the workplace to cheat their way through the course without actually learning. Again, these are not fatal objections but challenges worth considering

Perhaps the greatest challenge that MOOCs must overcome is the ivory towers of the entrenched higher education establishment. Low-cost, widely accessible MOOCs represent a serious existential threat to physical institutions that thrive on high tuition rates and expensive room-and-board programs. As we've seen with enterprises like Udacity, why would a student spend hundreds of thousands of dollars on tuition when he or she can get an education of the same caliber virtually free? Frankly, MOOCs could put inefficient, low-performing colleges and universities out of business. It's not surprising that the establishment has already begun to push back.

In October 2012, the state of Minnesota, citing a twenty-year-old state law requiring universities to get state approval for operation, banned Coursera from offering courses to Minnesota residents. The backlash from the public (thanks to the Internet, ironically) was swift and loud. Under a barrage of complaints, the Minnesota Office of Higher Education backed off the initial ruling and said that any Minnesotan should be able to utilize Coursera's and other MOOCs' free, online, noncredit courses. It was a short-lived victory for MOOCs, however, because Minnesota added that if Coursera started charging for the classes or offering credits or certificates, Minnesota would likely rethink its decision. Certainly, there will be more fights on the horizon for Coursera and other MOOCs.

The purpose of this book has been to expose the cold reality and empty rhetoric of much of college education in America. In this chapter we offered solutions to the various problems in higher education. We noted that America must improve its failing K–12 systems that send students to college ill prepared to succeed. Next, colleges and lenders must rein in the student-loan debt crisis and runaway tuition costs by stopping easy loans policies and pushing everyone to attend college. As we explained, not all students are suited to attend college nor are they needed to attend. We must develop and pursue more vocational and technical schools to fill the many valuable skilled jobs that are going begging today.

The most promising aspect of higher education is the explosion of MOOCs and comprehensive, online education. Whatever the ultimate success of initiatives like Udacity, one of the great hopes for online ventures is that they will increase the pressure on American postsecondary institutions for transparency and accountability.

New innovators, with new ideas, threaten an uncompromising group of underperforming colleges that are producing underqualified graduates who owe mountains of debt. If traditional higher education wants to retain its prestige, its historical significance, and its students, it should reestablish a college education as an investment that serves the heart, the mind, and the checkbook. If it doesn't, the future of higher education may move on without it. New challengers in technology and individual and corporate entrepreneurship, along with public dissatisfaction with the current state of higher education, may help us all focus better on our choices, not only as individuals and educational institutions but also as a community and a country.

Twelve Hypothetical Scenarios

Scenario #1

You went to a public high school and made the National Honor Society. You scored in the top 10 percent on your SATs and were president of student government. Your family can give you $15,000 per year to go to school, but you really like politics and have been accepted to Georgetown, a school that runs upward of $50,000. Your brother, who studied marketing, just moved back in with your parents after graduation, and he owes $40,000 in student-loan debt. You're scared of that situation, but you don't want to give up on a great opportunity that you've worked hard for.

Verdict: Cross your fingers that Georgetown can give you private grants or scholarships to help with the costs. If it doesn't, take a hard look at less-competitive, but less-expensive schools in the area. Especially if you think you one day might attend graduate school, it might not be the best thing to take out big loans on your BA. Plus, you can always snag an internship on the Hill for a summer. If you decide to go to Georgetown, hedge your bets: maybe double major in something that might make you some money after graduation, not land you a $32,000-per-year job at a think tank or news organization.

Scenario #2

You're a minority male living in the inner city. Your family (single mom) isn't destitute but doesn't have any real money to send you to college. You've worked pretty hard in high school to get where you are in the top 20 percent of the class. You see classmates with nicer clothes and more friends, but you know they don't work as hard or have as much desire to achieve as you do. Your guidance counselor has said that you have good odds of getting some Pell Grant money and non-loan grants and scholarships from schools. You're hoping that's true, but you're prepared to borrow anything to get ahead in life anyway. You want a career helping people like you, maybe being an English teacher.

Verdict: Definitely go to school. Since you're motivated to overcome long odds, you might even be comfortable borrowing more money than most people should. Aim high on your application to selective private schools, since they want to broaden their demographic pool of accepted students and often give money to do so. As a safety measure, find an academically strong large public school that might give you money purely on academic merit and the tuition will be more affordable to you.

SCENARIO #3

You've gone to a pretty good public high school or private school. Your parents make enough money that paying for college isn't an issue. You are set to graduate in the top 20 percent of your class and scored 2100 on your SAT. You're not 100 percent positive about what you want to study, but you've noticed that you enjoy reading about business and economics when you do pick up a newspaper. To you, going to college is important because you really want a good job that a college degree promises. Also, you're really looking forward to being around lots of girls, and when you visited your cousin's fraternity last summer, that seemed like a blast.

VERDICT: You should probably go, but largely because your mom and dad can pay for school—a huge financial advantage for you. You might not become a famous economist, but you might have an interest or talent for numbers and business. Just make sure your grades don't get dragged down by too much partying. A lower GPA will make you less competitive to top firms when it comes time to get a job.

SCENARIO #4

You're a B-student in a middle-class family, and your favorite class in high school was History through Film. Most days after school, you're catching up on *Call of Duty*. Dad is always on your case about not "reaching your potential." It's assumed you will go to college, and Mom and Dad can help somewhat. Still, you're fine with borrowing $10,000 per year to go, since you won't have to pay it off until, like, ten years from now or something. You can't wait to go to college, since Mom is such a drag with her nagging, and you can't wait to get away to school and let loose a little bit.

Verdict: Your priorities are off. Are you really prepared to borrow a lot of money when the main goal is drinking beers? Are you really excited to learn, or do you just want to get a piece of paper so somebody can give you a job? A better bet would be to do a year of community college or commute to a state school and save some money, if possible. Lower the stakes on your academic bets before you decide to commit $40,000 per year. Tough out another year at home, and put down the video games.

Scenario #5

In high school, you did well in subjects that interested you and got Cs and Ds in the ones that didn't. College has always been on your radar because you really want to study European history. Last year, you won a prize for an essay you wrote for English class. You've gotten into some good private schools because of your decent GPA, but you didn't get any scholarship money because of bad grades in math and science. Your family is ready to give you $20,000 per year for school, and you want to honor that investment and do well. You really want a good liberal arts education and can't wait to soak up the Great Books. As for career, you're confident something will work out, even if you study liberal arts. You think it's probably worth it to borrow $12,000 per year, since you're smart enough to land a good job and pay back that debt. Plus, everyone else is borrowing, so it can't be that dumb a move.

VERDICT: A classic college trap. You don't realize that not every liberal arts college teaches the liberal arts in the way you want. You may be overstating your own abilities. Why should you take out lots of loans when you couldn't get by high school geometry? You're also overstating the value of a private school education. Save yourself and your parents some money, and go to a big state school, which often has a broader and more orthodox curriculum than little private schools. Learn discipline for things you don't like to do.

SCENARIO #6

You do so-so in school but really enjoy being around cars and getting your hands dirty while working on them. You feel pressured to go away to school just because lots of your friends are doing it, but you don't really like to sit and do homework or be in class. On the other hand, you don't want to be thought of as a dumb kid who went to community college or trade school, and you have some talent for math and science. You know you could get in *somewhere*, but you would probably just go to the cheapest place you and your family could afford. You don't want to be like your sister with $60,000 in loans for a fine arts degree.

VERDICT: Don't succumb to peer pressure! In a few years, you won't ever talk to 95 percent of the people you went to high school with, so don't worry about conforming to their expectations. If it's a smart move financially, enroll in a good trade school or community college. If you really like stripping and rebuilding engines, odds are you will find great satisfaction in your work, something you can't put a price tag on. Plus, mechanics get *paid*, their work can't be outsourced, and you can always give a four-year degree a shot later.

SCENARIO #7

Even though you're seventeen, you developed an iPhone app for your senior project in computer science. Now you've been accepted to MIT. You know you'll get an awesome education and be around lots of smart people there, but the high price tag is holding you back, even though your parents are willing to give you $18,000 per year. Stanford and Princeton have also accepted you, but they are also over $50,000 per year. It just doesn't seem worth it to spend that for a BA.

VERDICT: It doesn't seem worth it, but in your case, it might be. You've already shown some real talent and initiative for what you're interested in. That will take you far in life. Also, top schools are often eager to give away need-based grants to help cover the costs of attendance. You've got a good shot to get some of that money. Plus, most grads in STEM disciplines at top schools like MIT, Princeton, and Stanford can come out of school and make good salaries at software companies, hedge funds, or research laboratories at top corporations. Spend the money, and keep working hard.

The other option for you is to try and enter the workforce right away. You've already got a small portfolio of work for a company to review. If you get hired, continue your education by taking MOOCs, and rack up free credentials in college-level programming courses from MIT and Harvard! Especially in the tech sector, it's important to establish what you can do, not show a piece of paper. Apply that knowledge to your work.

SCENARIO #8

You're homeschooled and really want to be a veterinarian. Your grades and SATs can get you into places like Tufts, George Washington, Villanova, and Williams, but living as a Christian is also really important to you, and you aren't eager to be around the typical dorm environment. Moreover, you're politically conservative and don't feel that sitting in a liberal classroom is a good use of your time or brain. You've heard about places like Grove City, Patrick Henry, University of Dallas, and Union University, but you don't know if their academic reputations will impress when it comes time to apply for graduate school.

VERDICT: Don't take out big loans or make your parents pay huge money for an experience you don't really want. If a Christian environment is important to you, prioritize that above all else. One of the great things about small religiously affiliated schools is that their costs of attendance are usually relatively low. If you've got to pay for veterinary school later (a pricey choice), it might be prudent to spend a lot less for your BA. Assuming you've got good grades, standardized test scores are of great importance in graduate admission, regardless of your field. Do excellently on those, and you'll greatly improve your chances of getting into the school you want, regardless of where your BA is from.

Scenario #9

You're thirty-three, a single mom with two young kids. You are able to pay the bills as a nurse, but things are getting tighter. You want to get a leg up on your career and earn some more money by getting an MA in health care management. Your schedule is already crazy enough as it is, so going to class every day doesn't seem like an option. You could do it if you enrolled in one of those online universities, but you know somebody who went for two semesters and dropped out because, according to her, she wasn't learning anything, and it was pretty expensive. At this stage of life, you don't have any room for financial mistakes.

Verdict: A for-profit online university could be a good option, but explore online programs at nonprofit universities, too, if only because they might have a little more name recognition to employers. Check out Western Governors University's online program; the people there can pair you with an individualized career counselor to help you make the best decisions, and you can test out of courses you might not need to take. If you're really terrified of committing to a full

MA program because of the cost, see if you can get a certificate somewhere to boost your credentials.

SCENARIO #10

You never took high school that seriously and did just enough to graduate. Everything was hard or boring. A year later, you're still living at home and working as a roofer. You have a little money in your pocket now, but you're starting to feel like life is passing you by a little bit. After work, you like to come home and watch UFC and smoke pot with your bros. Going to college really doesn't interest you and you don't have money for it, but you don't want to be working on a roof forever.

VERDICT: Take a hard look at the military. You've already shown you have the ability to work outside doing manual labor all day, so you aren't a total weakling. It's a good place to get skills and discipline without spending a ton of money for the education. If you want to do some school later on, you can do online courses to get a degree while you stay in the service. But be prepared to make hard sacrifices and build physical and mental toughness. And stop smoking pot or you won't be eligible.

SCENARIO #11

You've won some prizes in competitions for photography and graphic design, and people are always praising your artistic talent. But you have ADD and some clinical anxiety and depression issues, and you don't easily connect with people. As a consequence, your grades in high school were usually Bs and Cs. Going away to college seems to be a scary social experiment, and you aren't confident you are academically prepared to do well. Your parents earn a lot of money, so paying for it isn't an issue, but you're not sure it's the best choice.

VERDICT: Definitely try community college first, even if you have to take remedial courses. Starting at college can be a tough experience socially. Don't put yourself into that situation if you don't feel ready for it. Take classes close to home in what you want to do. If classes go well and your mental state improves, think about transferring to a four-year school later on. In any case, keep looking for gigs to expose your work. In the art world, a degree is very helpful but not essential.

SCENARIO #12

You were an average student at a poor-performing public high school in California. Biology was your best subject. All of your friends are working fast-food jobs or living off their moms. You think you need to go to college to get a good job, so you're considering going to community college. You have no resources—going to school full-time just isn't an option, and many people in your poor neighborhood think you are a "sellout" for wanting an education. Since you had average grades in high school, you're discouraged by having to enroll in some remedial courses right off the bat. After all, that's a ton of money and time.

Verdict: Enroll in community college part-time. MOOC (Massive Online Open Course) programs are being developed for community colleges in California, so at some point you may be able to take classes online for reduced cost. Since you're only going part-time, find a job to work at while you do school—at this point in your life it is important to build work experience. If you work hard, you can get a job with only an associate's degree in one of the hard or applied sciences. Make this your goal at all costs.

Schools Worth Attending

The following are schools which the authors believe deserve attention. Certainly they are not the only schools worthy of possible attendance. Many others like them merit a student's time and investment. We list these to illustrate that there is a broad range of worthwhile institutions in higher education.

Religious Schools

Biola University: Biola University is an evangelical school located 20 minutes from downtown Los Angeles. It is a draw for students who take their faith seriously but also desire to work in the entertainment industry. All students are required to take 30 credit hours of Bible classes, and its Torrey Honors (Great Books) program is also well regarded.

Catholic University of America: Catholic University offers a traditional Catholic approach to student life, a strong liberal arts program, and an overall better value than some other similarly priced schools in the DC area.

Franciscan University of Steubenville: Franciscan University of Steubenville (OH) has built a curriculum around the staples of Catholic learning, offering majors like catechetics, classics, and sacred music, in addition to vocational concentrations like nursing and an engineering program starting in fall 2013. Franciscan also lives out Catholic teaching on social issues, as it has challenged the federal government in court over the onerous Obamacare HHS mandate.

Grove City College: This Pennsylvania institution has a biblical worldview, engaged students (44 percent of freshmen graduated in the top 10 percent of their high school class), and the right price (roughly $22,000 per year).

Mississippi College (Clinton): Mississippi College is a Christian school with a great core curriculum, offering mandatory classes in, among other subjects, lab science, Bible, English, and history. BA candidates must also take 12 credits of a foreign language. Mississippi College's tuition is about $14,000 per year, a relative bargain.

Patrick Henry College: Patrick Henry is a popular destination for the nation's smartest homeschoolers with a close proximity to Washington, DC, and reasonable tuition (about $24,000 per year) for a Christian liberal arts education.

University of Dallas: With a small student body that builds relationships, a Jesuit approach to a traditional liberal arts education, and a great price tag (around $20,000 per year) the University of Dallas offers a solid education at a price you can't beat.

The Elites

University of Chicago: The University of Chicago is a distinguished private university known around the world for its scientific and academic research. It is the origin of the Chicago school of economics and the home to many highly distinguished alumni. Its business, law, and public policy postgraduate schools are among the most highly respected in the country.

Harvard University: The most elite university in the world still commands respect from employers on its name alone. It offers some of the absolute best career networking opportunities and some of the most eminent instructors in the world.

Princeton: Princeton is still one of the best schools academically in the Ivy League. Unlike some of the other elite universities, Princeton emphasizes undergraduate education. Like Harvard, it provides great career networking opportunities and even offers several academic programs for political conservatives.

Stanford University: Stanford is one of the world's leading research institutions. With its tremendous faculty, beautiful campus, and terrific undergraduate student body, it's been arguably the most prominent feeder school to Silicon Valley's most successful entrepreneurs and startup companies.

Technical and Engineering Schools

Colorado School of Mines: With very rigorous STEM programs, the Colorado School of Mines is geared especially toward producing graduates to work immediately in the very lucrative energy industry.

Cooper Union: Located in downtown Manhattan, Cooper Union is by definition an elite university, as students qualified enough to enroll pay nothing to attend. The institution provides some of the best STEM programs not just in the country but in the world.

Georgia Tech: One of the top schools in the country for return on investment, it boasts top-notch engineering programs and lots of opportunities to connect with local companies looking for emerging talent.

Rice University: Rice offers some of the best STEM programs in the country, hands down. The small student body means lots of contact with professors. Located in Houston, Texas, Rice graduates are met with plentiful job opportunities and excellent return on investment.

Texas A&M: Texas A&M offers first-class STEM programs at a very agreeable price tag for in-state students.

Virginia Polytechnic Institute and State University (VA Tech): Virginia Tech produces graduates well-equipped to succeed in the hard sciences, and at an attractive price for tuition. Tech also has a flourishing internship and co-op educational program, providing students with opportunities to gain work experience.

WyoTech: Primarily concentrating on training students in automotive maintenance skills, WyoTech also offers education in HVAC, plumbing, and electrical work. Their facility in Laramie, Wyoming, is particularly impressive, although WyoTech has several campuses around the country. WyoTech also makes serving and instructing veterans a priority.

State Schools

George Mason University: Offering a great price tag for Virginians and close proximity to the jobs and internships of Washington, DC, George Mason is a worthwhile investment.

Nova Southeastern: Nova Southeastern has a sterling reputation in the South Florida area, offering a competitive tuition rate for roughly 175 different majors. In recent years, Nova has grown increasingly selective in its admissions, despite enrolling over 11,000 undergraduates. Its College of Allied Health and Sciences is particularly strong. Its multiple campuses and online offerings are also attractive to working students.

Rutgers–New Brunswick: With high return on investment and close proximity to New York City, Rutgers offers students many quality internships and job opportunities.

San Jose State University: We mention SJSU for their pilot program with California-based Udacity, a company using the Internet to expand and cheapen higher education. Required math classes will be offered to matriculated and nonmatriculated students for only $150. As a feeder school for Silicon Valley tech companies, SJSU is continuing to produce graduates that the economy needs.

University of Illinois–Urbana–Champaign: For a state school, the University of Illinois–Urbana–Champaign boasts above-average ROI numbers and a huge diversity of majors.

University of California–San Diego: This is ranked one of the best-value schools on our list in terms of return on investment, and the retail factor of living in San Diego isn't too bad either.

University of Michigan: The University of Michigan features many academically rigorous programs, especially in engineering disciplines, a solid return on investment, and one of the storied college football programs.

University of Texas–Austin: Besides one of the best college sports atmospheres in the country (for when you're not studying), the University of Texas–Austin is very affordable and offers a huge diversity of subjects to major in. If you're a creative type, you won't have a shortage of outlets for your work in Austin.

Western Governors University: WGU is an online, non-profit university that is committed to its students finishing their degrees in ways that are as timely and debt-free as possible. Because WGU offers majors in only a few disciplines, the quality of instruction is high. It has partnered with state university systems.

William and Mary: A competitively priced public school for both in-state and out-of-state students, William and Mary offers a high level of name recognition to employers and proven historical pedigree.

Private Schools

Amherst College: If you don't mind spending big money on a Northeast liberal arts college outside the Ivy League with a palpable liberal atmosphere, this is the school for you. For a liberal arts school, it offers a great ROI, despite its pricey up-front cost and trendy and definite left-wing orientation.

Baylor University (Waco, TX): Baylor offers a huge diversity of majors, and was one of only twenty-one schools (out of more than 1,000) to receive an "A" rating from the American Council of Trustees and

Alumni for teaching core subjects. Accepting roughly 40 percent of its applicants, Baylor is quite robust, and its ROI is fairly high as well.

Furman University: Outside the most competitive liberal arts universities in the South (Duke and Emory), Furman has an impressive record of graduate achievement and decent ROI. It comes with a steep price tag, however.

Hillsdale College: Hillsdale is one of the few liberal arts institutions committed to a conservative, liberal arts education grounded in the classics of Western heritage. Hillsdale has a rich history of conservative tradition and is one of the few colleges that require all of its students to study the U.S. Constitution as part of the core curriculum.

Howard University: For students seeking a traditional black college, Howard University has a rich and noteworthy history. Its proximity to Washington D.C. offers students valuable connections to political networks and jobs in government. Its return on investment is above average and competitive with earnings of graduates from the University of Oregon and University of Vermont, according to Payscale.com data.

Newberry College (Newberry, SC): Building their school in the context of traditional values, Newberry primarily conducts education in the liberal arts, though staples like accounting, biology, chemistry, and nursing majors are also available. For those considering signing up for an ROTC program,

Newberry also has a Military Science Leadership minor. Newberry also shows some financial responsibility to its students, as the school recently decided to freeze tuition for all four years for members of the 2013 freshman class.

Spellman College: Spellman College is a historically black, four-year women's college located in Atlanta, Georgia. It boasts a rigorous liberal arts program and a distinguished field of alumnae. Upon invitation from the college and Mrs. Martin Luther King, coauthor Bennett lectured there in 1986.

St. Vincent College: Set in one of the most scenic areas of Pennsylvania, St. Vincent College also offers a rigorous liberal arts curriculum, with particularly strong programs in politics and theology. St. Vincent College also offers generous scholarships for undergraduates: a 3.0 GPA and 1000+ on the SAT will qualify you for $15,000 per year.

The Military Academies

The Army (West Point), Navy (Annapolis), Coast Guard, and Air Force academies have forged character, intellect, and heroism for generations. Enrolling in one of the four academies of the US military fulfills one of the highest callings of service to the nation, as well as the assurance of academic and physical challenges. The cost of attendance is free, and the education is excellent, but personal sacrifices will be made.

For-Profits

Grand Canyon University (Phoenix): A high-integrity school coming from a faith-based values system, GCU embraces technology, focuses on creative ways to make education more accessible, is tuition sensitive, and treats students as customers.

DeVry University: DeVry has locations all over the country, and it strives to be the best in niche disciplines like business, IT, and engineering. A BA is possible in three years of full-time study. DeVry has a great track record of producing graduates, and it has strong leadership as well.

Full Sail University: Full Sail also has campuses in several locations, and it has world-class facilities and instructors for training students in the technical arts. Offering mainly twelve-month diploma programs and eighteen-month associate degrees, they are a major feeder school for the music business (Nashville), the video game industry (California), and film (New York). Graduates of Full Sail get hired.

Acknowledgments

This book is more than the output of two individuals. Many hands were lifted to make it happen. Accordingly, there are a number of individuals to whom credit must be given.

Joel Miller, a gifted editor and patient shepherd of this project, as well as the rest of the staff at Thomas Nelson.

Brian Kennedy and the support of the Claremont Institute, where real classical education and inquiry takes place every day among its scholars, programs for young fellows, and on the pages of the Claremont Review of Books.

Christopher Beach, a good man and a good friend. We are grateful for your contributions, editing, and guidance throughout this project.

Noreen Burns, an invaluable source of assistance in all matters great and small. Thank you for serving us both so well every day. Claude Jennings, a daily source of encouragement, calm, and good humor.

Our friend Seth Leibsohn, who is always eager to offer help and advice in all situations. Nathan Martin, witty in himself, and the cause of wit in others.

Sarah Danaher, Chris Herndon, and Dan Nassimbene.

Thanks for taking the time to sit for interviews. All best to your families.

Sebastian Thrun and Peter Thiel, whose vision for improving higher education was a source of inspiration.

Charles Murray, who offered helpful remarks on the manuscript.

Richard Vedder, whom we relied on for perspective and information, and Andrew Gillen, for the same.

Checker Finn, David Gelernter, Steven Hayward, Kathryn-Jean Lopez, James Pethokoukis, and Nick Schulz, friends and first-rate thinkers. We are glad America has you.

Lastly, all of the *Morning in America* listeners who help shape our thinking and our country. You are never taken for granted.

BILL:

My loving companion and wife, Elayne, for whom her honor is her strength, and dignity her clothing. Thank you for 30 years of love and support.

My sons, John and Joe. It brings me great pride and joy to see how you have made your way in the world.

To my late friend Brooke Williams. I miss you on the island, but you're never far from my thoughts. I am grateful for our years of friendship.

DAVID:

The Lamb of God, Jesus Christ, who takes away the sin of the world.

My mom and dad, my first teachers, who always believed in me. You are both heroes of mine.

My brother Zack. I wouldn't have wanted to grow up with anyone else.

My sister Melanie. I'm in awe of your accomplishments. You've got an amazing future ahead of you.

My dear friends Nathan and Shona Martin. A daily blessing to my personal, professional, and spiritual life.

Sam and Jaime Arora, Drew Bratcher, Jeff Durkin, Will Fleeson, and Andy Walker. Faithful friends all.

Mr. Brian A. King, my first Latin teacher and progenitor of my adult intellectual life.

My friends and colleagues of the Claremont Institute.

My colleagues and professors at the CUA Department of Greek and Latin.

Notes

The Truth about College

1. *Good Will Hunting*, 1997, Be Gentlemen Limited Partnership, "Memorable Quotes," IMDb.com, http://www.imdb.com/title/tt0119217/quotes.
2. Jordan Weissmann, "53% of Recent College Grads Are Jobless or Underemployed—How?" *Atlantic*, April 23, 2012, http://www.theatlantic.com/business/archive/2012/04/53-of-recent-college-grads-are-jobless-or-underemployed-how/256237/.
3. Anthony Carnevale, Nicole Smith, et al., "Help Wanted: Projections of Jobs and Education Requirements Through 2018," Georgetown University Center on Education and the Workforce, June 2010, 14, http://cew.georgetown.edu/jobs2018/.
4. ACICS, "Survey on Workplace Skills Preparedness," Fact Sheet, November 2011, http://www.acics.org/events/content.aspx?id=4718.

Introduction

1. Josh Mitchell and Maya Jackson-Randall, "Student-Loan Debt Tops $1 Trillion," *Wall Street Journal*, March 22, 2012.
2. Frank Bruni, "The Imperiled Promise of College," *New York Times*, April 28, 2012, http://www.nytimes.com/2012/04/29/opinion/sunday/bruni-the-imperiled-promise-of-college.html.

Chapter 1: The Borrowing Binge

1. Kayla Webley, "Woman with Asperger's Dodges Bullet on Nearly $340,000 in Student Loans," *Time*, May 30, 2012, http://newsfeed.time.com/2012/05/30/woman-with-aspergers-dodges-bullet-on-nearly-340000-in-student-loans/.
2. Authors' personal interview, May 6, 2012.
3. Jonathan Liang, "What a Drag!" *Barron's*, April 16, 2012, http://online.barrons.com/article/SB50001424053111904857404577333842637459600.html.
4. Andrew Martin and Andrew Lehren, "A Generation Hobbled by the Soaring Cost of College," *New York Times*, May 12, 2012, http://www.nytimes.com/2012/05/13/business/student-loans-weighing-down-a-generation-with-heavy-debt.html?pagewanted=all.
5. US Department of Education, National Center for Education Statistics, 2007–08 National Postsecondary Student Aid Study, http://nces.ed.gov/das/library/tables_listings/showTable2005.asp?popup=true&tableID=4610&rt=p.
6. Meta Brown, Andrew Haughwout, et al., "Grading Student Loans," *Federal Reserve Quarterly Report on Household Debt and Credit*, March 5, 2012, http://libertystreeteconomics.newyorkfed.org/2012/03/grading-student-loans.html.
7. US Department of Education, "Fast Facts," http://nces.ed.gov/fastfacts/display.asp?id=98.
8. Pew Research, "1 in 5 Households Now Owe Student Loan Debt," September 26, 2012, http://pewresearch.org/pubs/2369/student-debt-record-number-households-owe-young-poor-college-university.
9. Jenna Johnson, "One Trillion Dollars: Student Loan Debt Builds Toward Yet Another Record," *Washington Post*, October 19, 2011, http://www.washingtonpost.com/blogs/campus-overload/post/one-trillion-dollars-student-loan-debt-builds-toward-yet-another-record/2011/10/19/gIQAbUoJyL_blog.html.
10. Mark Kantrowitz, "Total College Debt Now Exceeds Total

Credit Card Debt," FastWeb.org, August 11, 2010, http://www.fastweb.com/financial-aid/articles/2589-total-college-debt-now-exceeds-total-credit-card-debt.

11. "This Year's Freshmen at 4-Year Colleges, Highlights of a Survey," *Chronicle of Higher Education*, January 21, 2010, http://chronicle.com/article/This-Years-Freshmen-at-4-Year/63672/.
12. Olivier Knox, "Obama: I Only Paid Off My Student Loans Eight Years Ago," ABCNews.com, April 24, 2012, http://abcnews.go.com/Politics/OTUS/obama-paid-off-student-loans-years-ago/story?id=16204817#.T6mDlY6G8y4.
13. Liang, "What a Drag!"
14. Melanie Hunter, "More Than 15% Still Paying Back Student Loans at Age 50," Catholic News Service, May 4, 2012, http://cnsnews.com/news/article/more-15-percent-still-paying-back-student-loans-age-50.
15. Amanda M. Fairbanks, "Seeking Arrangement: College Students Using 'Sugar Daddies' to Pay Off Student Loan Debt," *Huffington Post*, July 7, 2011, http://www.huffingtonpost.com/2011/07/29/seeking-arrangement-college-students_n_913373.html.
16. Catherine Rampell, "Outlook Is Bleak Even for Recent College Graduates," *New York Times*, May 18, 2011, http://www.nytimes.com/2011/05/19/business/economy/19grads.html.
17. Ruth Simon and Michael Corkery, "Cost of College: Push to Gauge Bang for Buck From College Gains Steam," *Wall Street Journal*, February 11, 2013. http://online.wsj.com/article/SB10001424127887324880504578298162378392502.html
18. Nathaniel Penn, "Hello, Cruel World," *New York Times*, May 29, 2012, http://www.nytimes.com/2012/03/25/magazine/what-the-fate-of-one-class-of-2011-says-about-the-job-market.html/?pagewanted=all.
19. Frank Bruni, "The Imperiled Promise of College," *New York Times*, April 28, 2012, emphasis ours, http://www

.nytimes.com/2012/04/29/opinion/sunday/bruni-the-imperiled-promise-of-college.html.

20. Ibid.
21. Rampell, "Outlook Is Bleak."
22. Mark Cuban, "The Coming Meltdown in College Education and Why the Economy Won't Get Better Anytime Soon," *Mark Cuban Weblog*, May 12, 2012, http://blogmaverick.com/2012/05/13/the-coming-meltdown-in-college-education-why-the-economy-wont-get-better-any-time-soon/.
23. American Student Assistance, FinAid.org, "Student Loan Debt Statistics," http://www.asa.org/policy/resources/stats/default.aspxhttp://www.finaid.org/loans/ (accessed January 7, 2012).
24. Bonnie Kavoussi, "Number of PhD Recipients Using Food Stamps Surged During Recession: Report," *Huffington Post*, May 8, 2012, http://www.huffingtonpost.com/2012/05/07/food-stamps-phd-recipients-2007-2010_n_1495353.html#s609260&title=10_South_Carolina.
25. Ibid.
26. Leonard Cassuto, "Grad Student Debt Matters," *Chronicle of Higher Education*, November 20, 2011, http://chronicle.com/article/Graduate-Student-Debt-Matters/129812/.
27. Joe Palazzolo, "Law Grads Face Brutal Job Market," *Wall Street Journal*, June 25, 2012, http://online.wsj.com/article/SB10001424052702304458604577486623469958142.html#project%3DLSCHOOL20120625%26articleTabs%3Dinteractive.
28. Elizabeth Lesly Stevens, "Will Law School Students Have Jobs After They Graduate?" *Washington Post*, October 31, 2012, http://www.washingtonpost.com/lifestyle/magazine/will-law-school-students-have-jobs-after-they-graduate/2012/10/31/f9916726-0f30-11e2-bd1a-b868e65d57eb_story.html.
29. US Bureau of Labor Statistics, "College Enrollment and Work Activity of 2011 High School Graduates," press release, April 19, 2012, http://www.bls.gov/news.release/hsgec.nr0.htm.
30. Naomi Schaefer Riley, "What Is a College Education Really

Worth?" *Washington Post*, June 3, 2011, http://www.washingtonpost.com/opinions/what-is-a-college-education-really-worth/2011/06/02/AGzIO4HH_story.html.

31. Charles Murray, "What's Wrong with Vocational School?" *Wall Street Journal*, January 17, 2007, http://www.aei.org/article/society-and-culture/citizenship/whats-wrong-with-vocational-school/.
32. US secretary of education Arne Duncan, remarks at White House Press Conference, April 20, 2012, http://www.whitehouse.gov/the-press-office/2012/04/20/press-briefing-press-secretary-jay-carney-and-secretary-education-arne-d.
33. Martin and Lehren, "A Generation Hobbled."
34. Sallie Mae, "How America Pays for College 2011," August 14, 2011, https://docs.google.com/viewer?a=v&q=cache:gf0zmxAblKMJ:https://www1.salliemae.com/NR/rdonlyres/BAF36839-4913-456E-8883-ACD006B950A5/14952/HowAmericaPaysforCollege_2011.pdf+&hl=en&gl=us&pid=bl&srcid=ADGEESjqMxmixHufpPyF-bzRAR72c3clXIEwWhOCSWsJnFq_w5YO3E2WvtJyqPBYgewH4xKrb4KvgaPL4bQvUp5yOR1vP2fTUg9ebyHQqf6e5otk2KEqGphP8VABZvKGHtQ8-qGPh1ET&sig=AHIEtbTiDI5uj7f_-0my9oKKJ4idPs8YBw.
35. Pew Research Center, "Millennials: Confident, Connected, Open to Change," white paper issued February 24, 2010, 27, http://www.pewsocialtrends.org/2010/02/24/millennials-confident-connected-open-to-change/.
36. US Department of Education, National Center for Education Statistics, *Digest of Education Statistics, 2011* (NCES 2012-001), http://nces.ed.gov/fastfacts/display.asp?id=76.
37. Liang, "What a Drag!"
38. Martin and Lehren, "A Generation Hobbled."
39. "Institutions Charging More than 50K for Tuition, Fees, Room, and Board," *Chronicle of Higher Education*, October 26, 2011, http://chronicle.com/article/Sortable-Table-Institutions/129527/.

40. William J. Bennett, "Stop Subsidizing Soaring College Costs," CNN.com, March 22, 2012, http://www.cnn.com/2012/03/22/opinion/bennett-college-costs/index.html.
41. "Rising College Tuition: Students Struggle with Astronomical Increases," *Montgomery Advertiser*, August 16, 2012, http://recessionreality.blogspot.com/2012/08/rising-college-tuition-students.html.
42. Sallie Mae, "How America Pays for College 2011," August 9, 2011, https://docs.google.com/viewer?a=v&q=cache:gf0zmxAblKMJ:https://www1.salliemae.com/NR/rdonlyres/BAF36839-4913-456E-8883-ACD006B950A5/14952/HowAmericaPaysforCollege_2011.pdf+&hl=en&gl=us&pid=bl&srcid=ADGEESjqMxmixHufpPyF-bzRAR72c3clXIEwWhOCSWsJnFq_w5Y-O3E2WvtJyqPBYgewH4xKrb4KvgaPL4bQvUp5yOR-1vP2fTUg9ebyHQqf6e5otk2KEqGphP8VABZvKGHtQ8-qGPh1ET&sig=AHIEtbTiDI5uj7f_-0my9oKKJ4idPs8YBw.
43. Ibid., 10.
44. Ibid., 9.
45. Ibid.
46. Martin and Lehren, "A Generation Hobbled," Comments section.
47. Tyler Kingkade, "Student Loan Debt Sours Public Opinion on College Degrees' Worth, Consumers Prioritize Retirement Savings Instead: Survey," *Huffington Post*, July 18, 2012, http://www.huffingtonpost.com/2012/07/18/student-loans-debt-is-college-worth-it_n_1683083.html.
48. Martin and Lehren, "A Generation Hobbled."
49. Sue Shellenbarger, "To Pay Off Loans, Grads Put Off Marriage, Children," *Wall Street Journal*, April 17, 2012, http://online.wsj.com/article/SB10001424052702304818404577350030559887086.html.
50. Ibid.
51. Martin and Lehren, "A Generation Hobbled."
52. Ibid.

53. Brown, Haughwout, et al., "Grading Student Loans."
54. Meg Handley, "Are Student Loans the Next Debt Bomb?" *U.S. News and World Report*, February 8, 2012, http://www.usnews.com/news/articles/2012/02/08/are-student-loans-the-next-debt-bomb.
55. Martin and Lehren, "A Generation Hobbled."
56. James Pethokoukis, "Why Student Loans Might Be the Next Recipient of a Taxpayer Bailout," *AfEIdeas* (blog), November 28, 2012, http://www.aei-ideas.org/2012/11/why-student-loans-might-be-the-next-recipient-of-a-taxpayer-bailout/.

Chapter 2: Creating a Financial Monster

1. William J. Bennett, "Our Greedy Colleges," *New York Times*, February 18, 1987.
2. Lawrence Bowdish, "The Kids Aren't Alright: The Policymaking of Student Loan Debt," *eHistory Origins* 3, no 12 (September 2010), http://ehistory.osu.edu/osu/origins/article.cfm?articleid=44&articlepage=3&altcontent=no.
3. Andrew Martin and Andrew Lehren, "A Generation Hobbled by the Soaring Cost of College," *New York Times*, May 12, 2012, http://www.nytimes.com/2012/05/13/business/student-loans-weighing-down-a-generation-with-heavy-debt.html?pagewanted=all.
4. David M. Herszenhorn and Tamar Lewin, "Student Loan Overhaul Approved By Congress," *New York Times*, March 25, 2010, http://www.nytimes.com/2010/03/26/us/politics/26loans.html?_r=0 (accessed January 7, 2012).
5. Eileen Ambrose, "Student Loan Industry's 'Takeover' by Federal Government Is Overdue," *Baltimore Sun*, March 21, 2010, http://articles.baltimoresun.com/2010-03-21/business/bal-bz.ambrose21mar21_1_direct-lending-student-loan-student-aid/2.
6. Authors' e-mail exchange with Vedder, April 24, 2012.

7. "Loan Tradeoffs, Public vs. Private," FinAid.org., http://www.finaid.org/loans/loantradeoffs.phtml.
8. Ibid.
9. Editorial Board, "What College Students Need Most," *Washington Post*, April 29, 2012, http://www.washingtonpost.com/opinions/whats-better-for-college-students/2012/04/29/gIQA8kqKqT_story.html.
10. Kim Clark, "College Costs Climb, Yet Again," CNNMoney, October 29, 2011, http://money.cnn.com/2011/10/26/pf/college/college_tuition_cost/index.htm.
11. Ibid.
12. Current Inflation Rates: 2002–2012, US Inflation Calculator, http://www.usinflationcalculator.com/inflation/current-inflation-rates/.
13. Project on Student Debt, "State By State Data," October 18, 2012, http://projectonstudentdebt.org/state_by_state-data.php.
14. Douglas Holtz-Eakin, "#PleaseDoubleMyTerm" *National Review Online*, April 24, 2012, http://www.nationalreview.com/corner/296845/pleasedoublemyterm-douglas-holtz-eakin# (accessed January 7, 2013).
15. William J. Bennett, "Stop Subsidizing Soaring College Costs," CNN.com, March 22, 2012, http://articles.cnn.com/2012-03-22/opinion/opinion_bennett-college-costs_1_student-aid-financial-aid-tuition-at-public-universities?_s=PM:OPINION.
16. Ibid.
17. Ibid.
18. Ibid.
19. Josh Mitchell, "New Course in College Costs," *Wall Street Journal*, June 10, 2012, http://online.wsj.com/article/SB10001424052702303296604577454862437127618.html.
20. Tamar Lewin, "College May Become Unaffordable for Most in U.S.," *New York Times*, December 3, 2008, http://www.nytimes.com/2008/12/03/education/03college.html (accessed January 7, 2013).

21. Andrew Gillen, "Introducing Bennett Hypothesis 2.0," Center for College Affordability and Productivity White Paper, February 2012, 26, http://centerforcollegeaffordability.org/uploads/Introducing_Bennett_Hypothesis_2.pdf.
22. Stephanie Riegg Cellini and Claudia Goldin, "Does Federal Student Aid Raise Tuition? New Evidence on For-Profit Colleges," National Bureau of Economic Research Working Paper, February 2012, http://www.nber.org/papers/w17827.
23. Ibid., 2.
24. Mark Cuban, "The Coming Meltdown in College Education and Why the Economy Won't Get Better Anytime Soon," *Mark Cuban Weblog*, May 12, 2012, http://blogmaverick.com/2012/05/13/the-coming-meltdown-in-college-education-why-the-economy-wont-get-better-any-time-soon/.
25. "Biden Admits Government Subsidies Have Increased College Tuition," Real Clear Politics, February 6, 2012, http://www.realclearpolitics.com/video/2012/02/06/biden_admits_government_subsidies_have_increased_college_tuition.html.
26. Paul Kix, "Does Financial Aid Make College More Expensive?" *Boston Globe*, March 25, 2012, http://articles.boston.com/2012-03-25/ideas/31228641_1_financial-aid-federal-aid-college-tuitions/5.
27. Peter Wood cited in "Why They Seem to Rise Together, Student Aid and College Tuition," *Minding the Campus* (blog), February 20, 2012, emphasis added, http://www.mindingthecampus.com/originals/2012/02/why_they_seem_to_rise_together.html.
28. Gillen, "Introducing Bennett 2.0," 7.
29. "Pell Grants Flunk Out," *Wall Street Journal*, June 17, 2012.
30. Richard Vedder, "Why Liberals Should Want Spending on Colleges," Minding the Campus, http://www.mindingthecampus.com/originals/2013/02/why_liberals_should_want_less_.html (accessed February 10, 2013).

31. Bennett, "Stop Subsidizing Soaring College Costs."
32. Walter Russell Mead, "Eating the Poor: The College Debt Trap," *Via Meadia*, November 26, 2012, http://blogs.the-american-interest.com/wrm/2012/11/26/the-perverse-consequences-of-our-higher-ed-policy/.
33. Martin and Lehren, "A Generation Hobbled."
34. US Senate Health, Education, Labor and Pensions Committee, "The Return on the Federal Investment in For-Profit Education: Debt without a Diploma," report issued September 30, 2010, 9, http://www.harkin.senate.gov/documents/pdf/4caf6639e24c3.pdf.
35. Martin and Lehren, "A Generation Hobbled."
36. US Senate Committee, "Return on Federal Investment," 3.
37. Jonathan Liang, "What a Drag!" *Barron's*, April 16, 2012, http://online.barrons.com/article/SB50001424053111904857404577333842637459600.html.
38. Paul Fain, "Profiting from Federal Aid," *Inside Higher Ed*, February 14, 2012, http://www.insidehighered.com/news/2012/02/14/profits-receive-federal-aid-charge-more-study-finds.
39. Association of Private Sector Colleges and Universities, "Fact Sheet," http://www.career.org/iMISPublic/AM/Template.cfm?Section=About_CCA.
40. Ibid.
41. Martin and Lehren, "A Generation Hobbled."
42. Melissa Korn, "For-Profit Colleges Get Schooled," *Wall Street Journal*, October 24, 2012, http://online.wsj.com/article/SB10001424052970203937004578076942611172654.html
43. Testimony of Kathleen A. Bittel before the US Senate Health, Education, Labor, and Pensions Committee. "The Federal Investment in For-Profit Education: Are Students Succeeding?" September 30, 2010, http://www.help.senate.gov/hearings/hearing/?id=3e235bb6-5056-9502-5df5-5d5b0f000e01.
44. Libby A. Nelson, "Default Rates Continue Climb,

Mostly," *Inside Higher Ed*, October 1, 2012, http://www.insidehighered.com/news/2012/10/01/two-year-default-rates-student-loans-increase-again.

45. Martin and Lehren, "A Generation Hobbled."
46. Matthias Rieker, "Despite Concern, Banks Give Student Loans the Old College Try," *Wall Street Journal*, May 16, 2012, http://online.wsj.com/article/SB10001424052702304192704577406672529755652.html.
47. Karen Weise, "Private Student Loans Are Becoming More Competitive," *Businessweek*, May 23, 2012, http://www.businessweek.com/articles/2012-05-23/private-student-loans-are-becoming-more-competitive.
48. Rieker, "Despite Concern, Banks Give Student Loans the Old College Try."
49. Diana Jean Schemo, "Private Loans Deepen a Crisis in Student Debt," *New York Times*, June 10, 2007, http://www.nytimes.com/2007/06/10/us/10loans.html?pagewanted=all.
50. Ibid.
51. Ibid.
52. "Loan Tradeoffs, Public vs. Private," FinAid.org., http://www.finaid.org/loans/loantradeoffs.phtml.
53. Katrina Trinko, "Choose Your College, Major, and Loans Wisely," *USA Today*, April 22, 2012, http://www.usatoday.com/news/opinion/forum/story/2012-04-22/college-majors-student-loans/54474222/1.
54. William McGurn, "What's Your Kid Getting from College?" *Wall Street Journal*, November 1, 2011, http://online.wsj.com/article/SB10001424052970204394804577010080547122646.html.
55. Martin and Lehren, "A Generation Hobbled."
56. Peter J. Reilly, "Occupy Wall St.—We Need a Student Loan Bailout—But Let's March on the Colleges," *Forbes*, October 7, 2011, http://www.forbes.com/sites/peterjreilly/2011/10/07/occupy-wall-street-lets-have-a-student-loan-bailout-but-we-need-to-march-on-the-colleges/.

57. Richard Vedder, "Loans Are Part of the Problem, Not the Solution," *New York Times*, May 12, 2012, http://www.nytimes.com/roomfordebate/2012/05/12/easing-the-pain-of-student-loans/loans-are-part-of-the-problem-not-the-solution.
58. Michael Crow, "The Miseducation of American Dreamers," *Washington Post*, November 1, 2011, http://www.washingtonpost.com/national/on-leadership/the-miseducation-of-american-dreamers/2011/11/01/gIQAQ3B3cM_story.html.
59. Ronald J. Ostrow and Larry Gordon, "8 Ivy League Schools Sign Collusion Ban," *Los Angeles Times*, May 23, 1991, http://articles.latimes.com/1991-05-23/news/mn-3080_1_ivy-league-universities.
60. Malcolm Gladwell, "What College Rankings Really Tell Us," *New Yorker*, February 14, 2011, http://www.newyorker.com/reporting/2011/02/14/110214fa_fact_gladwell.
61. Ibid.
62. Martin and Lehren, "A Generation Hobbled."
63. Ibid.
64. Ron Lieber, "Placing the Blame as Students Are Buried in Debt," *New York Times*, May 28, 2010, http://www.nytimes.com/2010/05/29/your-money/student-loans/29money.html?pagewanted=all.
65. Ibid.
66. Bevonomics, http://www.bevonomics.org/.
67. Tamar Lewin, "Biden and College Presidents Talk About Paying the Bills," *New York Times*, June 5, 2012, http://www.nytimes.com/2012/06/06/education/obama-officials-aim-to-ease-college-cost-process.html?_r=2.
68. Joy Resmovitz, "Obama Addresses College Affordability, Tuition Costs in University of Michigan Speech," *Huffington Post*, January 27, 2012, http://www.huffingtonpost.com/2012/01/27/obama-to-target-rising-co_0_n_1236167.html.
69. Alex Pollock, "The Federal Home Loan Banks and Risk

Distribution in American Housing Finance," *Housing Finance International,* www.housingfinance.org/uploads/Publicationsmanager/0109_Fed.pdf.

70. Beth Pinsker Gladstone, "As College Costs Rise, Students Trade Dorm for Home: Sallie Mae," Reuters News Service reported in *Huffington Post,* July 16, 2012, http://www.huffingtonpost.com/2012/07/16/college-costs-rising-trade-dorm-for-home_n_1675132.html.
71. Monica Rohr, "Colleges Step Up Efforts to Stop Student Debt," *Houston Chronicle,* June 12, 2012, http://www.chron.com/news/houston-texas/article/Colleges-step-up-efforts-to-stop-student-debt-3623502.php.
72. See also Peter Thiel and the Thiel Fellowship later in chapter 3.
73. Luigi Zingales, "The College Graduate as Collateral," *New York Times,* June 13, 2012, http://www.nytimes.com/2012/06/14/opinion/the-college-graduate-as-collateral.html.
74. Peter Wood cited in "Why They Seem to Rise Together, Student Aid and College Tuition," *Minding the Campus.*
75. David Rubenstein, "Fat City," *Weekly Standard,* May 30, 2011, http://www.weeklystandard.com/print/articles/fat-city_567621.html.
76. Ibid.
77. Richard Vedder, Christopher Matgouranis, et al., "Faculty Productivity and Costs at the University of Texas at Austin," Center for College Affordability and Productivity Study, cited in "Data Shows Massive Disparity in Professor Productivity at UT Austin," PR Newswire, May 23, 2011, http://www.prnewswire.com/news-releases/data-shows-massive-disparity-in-professor-productivity-at-ut-austin-122448728.html.
78. Ibid.
79. Harry Jaffe, "Ben Ladner's Years of Living Lavishly," *Washingtonian* magazine, April 1, 2006, http://www.washingtonian.com/articles/people/ben-ladners-years-of-living-lavishly/.

80. Ibid.
81. Laura Bischoff, "OSU President Gee's Travel Bill Tops 800K," *Dayton Daily News*, May 6, 2012, http://www.daytondailynews.com/news/news/local/osu-president-gees-travel-bill-tops-800k/nNrW2/.
82. Martin and Lehren, "A Generation Hobbled."
83. Judy Lin, "California College Leaders Press for More Funding," *San Diego Tribune*, May 1, 2012, http://www.utsandiego.com/news/2012/may/01/california-college-leaders-press-for-more-funding/?print&page=all.
84. Kevin Kiley, "College Presidents' Paychecks Raise Brows," *Inside Higher Ed*, reprinted in *USA Today*, July 19, 2011, http://www.usatoday.com/news/education/2011-07-19-college-president-pay-increase_n.htm.
85. Lin, "California Leaders Press for More Funding."
86. Nanette Asimov, "UC President to Act on Executive Pension Demand," *San Francisco Chronicle*, March 28, 2012, http://www.sfgate.com/education/article/UC-president-to-act-on-executive-pension-demand-3438850.php.
87. Nanette Asimov, "UC Dean Christopher Edley Defends Pension Demands," *San Francisco Chronicle*, December 31, 2010, http://www.sfgate.com/education/article/UC-Dean-Christopher-Edley-defends-pension-demands-2451641.php.
88. Dick Vitale, "Sadly, Not Shocked By Sprewell's Comments," ESPN.com, November 8, 2004, http://espn.go.com/dickvitale/vcolumn041108-Sprewell.html.
89. Jay P. Greene, "Administrative Bloat at American Universities: The Real Reason for High Costs in Higher Education," *Goldwater Institute Policy Report*, no. 239, August 17, 2010, 1, http://goldwaterinstitute.org/article/administrative-bloat-american-universities-real-reason-high-costs-higher-education.
90. Ibid., 5.
91. Andrew Hacker and Claudia Dreifus, *Higher Education?* (New York: Holt and Company, 2010), 29.

92. Laurie Burkitt, "China to Cancel College Majors That Don't Pay," *Wall Street Journal*, November 23, 2011, http://blogs.wsj.com/chinarealtime/2011/11/23/china-to-cancel-college-majors-that-dont-pay/.
93. Martin and Lehren, "A Generation Hobbled."
94. "Colleges Adding High-Class Amenities," Foxboston.com, May 15, 2012, http://www.myfoxboston.com/story/18431183/2012/05/15/colleges-adding-high-class-amenities.
95. Carol Matlack, "Bubble U: High Point University," *Businessweek*, April 19, 2012, http://www.businessweek.com/printer/articles/22014-bubble-u-dot-high-point-university.
96. Chris Gigley, "University Transformed," *Sky*, January 2013.
97. Carol Matlack, "Bubble U: High Point University," *Businessweek*, April 19, 2012, http://www.businessweek.com/printer/articles/22014-bubble-u-dot-high-point-university.
98. Ibid.
99. Ibid.
100. Doug Lederman, "State Support Slumps Again," *Inside Higher Ed*, January 23, 2012, http://www.insidehighered.com/news/2012/01/23/state-funds-higher-education-fell-76-2011-12.

Chapter 3: So Is It Worth It?

1. *Good Will Hunting*, 1997, Be Gentlemen Limited Partnership, "Memorable Quotes," IMDb.com, http://www.imdb.com/title/tt0119217/quotes.
2. Mary Beth Marklein, "One Third of Young People Have a Bachelor's," *USA Today*, November 5, 2012, http://www.usatoday.com/story/news/nation/2012/11/05/college-graduates-pew/1683899/.
3. Anthony Carnevale, Nicole Smith, et al., "Help Wanted: Projections of Jobs and Education Requirements Through 2018," Georgetown University Center on Education and the Workforce, June 2010, 14, http://cew.georgetown.edu/jobs2018/.

4. US Census Bureau Current Population Survey, "Selected Measures of Household Income Dispersion: 1967 to 2010," www.census.gov/hhes/www/income/data/ . . . /inequality/IE-1.pdf.
5. Charles Murray, *Coming Apart: The State of White America, 1960–2010* (New York: Crown Forum, 2012), 61–63.
6. Transcript of President Barack Obama's Speech, February 24, 2009, http://www.whitehouse.gov/the_press_office/Remarks-of-President-Barack-Obama-Address-to-Joint-Session-of-Congress.
7. US secretary of education Arne Duncan, remarks at White House Press Conference, April 20, 2012, http://www.whitehouse.gov/the-press-office/2012/04/20/press-briefing-press-secretary-jay-carney-and-secretary-education-arne-d.
8. US Department of Education, "Percentage of 18–24 Year Olds Enrolled in Colleges and Universities," US Education Dashboard, http://dashboard.ed.gov/moreinfo.aspx?i=j&id=0&wt=0.
9. "The Big Payoff: Educational Attainment and Synthetic Estimates of Work-Life Earnings," US Census Bureau, July 2002, 4, http://www.census.gov/prod/2002pubs/p23-210.pdf.
10. Jack Hough, "College: 'Best Investment' or Big Risk?" Smartmoney.com, May 7, 2012, http://www.smartmoney.com/borrow/student-loans/college-best-investment-or-big-risk-1336353039981/.
11. US Department of Education, "Fast Facts," http://nces.ed.gov/fastfacts/display.asp?id=40 (accessed January 7, 2013).
12. Carnevale, Smith, et al., "Help Wanted: Projections of Jobs and Education Requirements Through 2018," 13.
13. Christine Armario, "Pathways to Prosperity Report: Students Need More Paths to Career Success," *Huffington Post*, February 2, 2011, http://www.huffingtonpost.com/2011/02/02/pathways-to-prosperity-re_n_817374.html.
14. Ibid.
15. Bureau of Labor Statistics, "High Wages After High School—Without a Bachelor's Degree," *BLS Occupational*

Outlook Quarterly, Summer 2012, 25–28, www.bls.gov/opub/ooq/2012/summer/art03.pdf.

16. Ibid., 28.
17. Ibid., 31.
18. Michael Morris, "Wanted: 10 Million Skilled Workers," *Washington Times*, November 9, 2011, http://www.washingtontimes.com/news/2011/nov/9/wanted-10-million-skilled-workers/.
19. Deloitte and the Manufacturing Institute, "Boiling Point?: The Skills Gap in US Manufacturing," 2011, 1–2, http://www.deloitte.com/assets/Dcom-UnitedStates/Local%20Assets/Documents/AD/us_PIP_2011SkillsGapReport_01142011.pdf.
20. Mike Rowe, "Written Testimony of Mike Rowe Before U.S. Senate Committee on Commerce, Science and Transportation," given May 11, 2011, http://www.mikeroweworks.com/2011/05/written-testimony-of-mike-rowe-before-u-s-senate-committee-on-commerce-science-and-transportation.
21. Robert Jonathan, "Dirty Jobs' Host Mike Rowe Sends Letter to Romney About Putting America Back to Work," *Inqusitr*, September 9, 2012, http://www.inquisitr.com/325596/dirty-jobs-host-mike-rowe-sends-letter-to-romney-about-putting-america-back-to-work/#swx83XMTXx81ucHB.99.
22. Leonard Sax, *Boys Adrift* (New York: Basic Books, 2007), 121–22.
23. Ibid.
24. Matthew Crawford, "The Case for Working with Your Hands," *New York Times*, May 21, 2009, http://www.nytimes.com/2009/05/24/magazine/24labor-t.html?pagewanted=all.
25. Bureau of Labor Statistics, "Occupational Employment and Wages, Electricians," May 2011, http://www.bls.gov/oes/current/oes472111.htm.
26. John W. Miller, "The $200,000-a-Year Mine Worker," *Wall Street Journal*, November 16, 2011, http://online.wsj.com/

article/SB10001424052970204621904577016172350869312.html?mod=WSJ_hp_us_mostpop_read.

27. Christine Armario, "Pathways to Prosperity Report: Students Need More Paths to Career Success," AP report in *Huffington Post*, February 2, 2011, http://www.huffingtonpost.com/2011/02/02/pathways-to-prosperity-re_n_817374.html.
28. Susan O'Doherty, "Who Is 'College Material'?" *Inside Higher Ed*, April 29, 2012, http://www.insidehighered.com/blogs/mama-phd/who-college-material.
29. Ibid.
30. Ibid.
31. Charles Murray, "Are Too Many People Going to College?" *American*, September 8, 2008, http://www.american.com/archive/2008/september-october-magazine/are-too-many-people-going-to-college.
32. Ibid.
33. Ibid.
34. Alex Tabarrok, "Tuning In to Dropping Out," *Chronicle of Higher Education*, June 4, 2012, http://chronicle.com/article/Tuning-In-to-Dropping-Out/130967/.
35. Ibid.
36. Ibid.
37. Stacey Patton, "The Ph.D. Now Comes with Food Stamps" *Chronicle of Higher Education*, May 13, 2012.
38. Crawford, "The Case for Working with Your Hands."
39. Ibid., emphasis added.
40. David Tonyan, "Bill Gates: Jobs Are Available, But Education System Is Failing," *The Daily Caller*, November 14, 2012, http://dailycaller.com/2012/11/14/bill-gates-jobs-are-available-but-education-system-is-failing/ (accessed January 7, 2013).
41. Ron Lieber, "Placing the Blame as Students Are Buried in Debt," *New York Times*, May 28, 2010, http://www.nytimes.com/2010/05/29/your-money/student-loans/29money.html?_r=1&hp=&adxnnl=1&adxnnlx=1275134734-Fpy4SBhQKxiUX8UGww0YjA.

42. Alex Tabarrok, "College Has Been Oversold," *Investor's Business Daily*, October 19, 2011, http://news.investors.com/article/588637/201110191813/college-has-been-oversold.htm.
43. Ibid.
44. Ibid.
45. Ibid.
46. Nick Schulz, "The Human Capital Imperative: Bringing More Minds to America," AmericanEnterpriseInstitute.com, January 31, 2012, http://www.aei.org/papers/society-and-culture/immigration/the-human-capital-imperative-bringing-more-minds-to-america2/.
47. PayScale College Salary Report, http://www.payscale.com/best-colleges/degrees.asp/.
48. For more on STEM education, we recommend Project Lead the Way, which provides middle and high schools with the training for productive STEM classes and curricula. Bennett is a senior advisor for Project Lead the Way. Go to www.PLTW.org.
49. Zac Anderson, "Rick Scott Wants to Shift University Funding Away from Some Degrees," *Miami Herald-Tribune*, October 10, 2011, http://politics.heraldtribune.com/2011/10/10/rick-scott-wants-to-shift-university-funding-away-from-some-majors/.
50. Ibid.
51. Laurie Burkitt, "China to Cancel College Majors That Don't Pay," *Wall Street Journal*, November 23, 2011, http://blogs.wsj.com/chinarealtime/2011/11/23/china-to-cancel-college-majors-that-dont-pay/.
52. Caitlin Dewey, "Worst College Majors for Your Career," Kiplinger.com, August 2012, http://www.kiplinger.com/slideshow/10-worst-college-majors-for-your-career/1.html#top.
53. Cited in Maurice Bremekamp, "Delta Airlines CEO Richard Anderson to Be New Metro Atlanta Chamber-Elect," *West Logistics*, October 23, 2012, http://www.westlgi.com/blog/.
54. Dominic J. Brewer, Eric R. Eide, et al., "Does It Pay

to Attend an Elite Private College?" *Journal of Human Resources* 34, no. 1 (Winter 1999): 104–23, http://www.jstor.org/stable/146304.

55. Mark Hoekstra, "The Effect of Attending the Flagship State University on Earnings: A Discontinuity-Based Approach," *Review of Economics and Statistics* 91, no. 4 (November 2009): 717–24.
56. Jere R. Behrman, Mark R. Rosenzweig, and Paul Taubman, "College Choice and Wages: Estimates Using Data on Female Twins," *Review of Economics and Statistics* 78, no. 4 (November 1996): 672–85, http://www.jstor.org/stable/2109954.
57. "2012 ROI Rankings: College Education Value Compared," PayScale.com, http://www.payscale.com/education/compare-college-costs-and-ROI.
58. "Methodology and Notes," PayScale.com, http://www.payscale.com/education/compare-college-costs-and-ROI.
59. Ibid.
60. Joe Richter, "Harvard Losing Out to South Dakota in Graduate Pay: Commodities," September 19, 2012, http://www.bloomberg.com/news/2012-09-17/harvard-losing-out-to-south-dakota-in-graduate-pay-commodities.html?cmpid=yhoo.
61. "2012 ROI Rankings: College Education Value Compared," PayScale.com.
62. "Bryn Mawr College," *U.S. News and World Report*, http://colleges.usnews.rankingsandreviews.com/best-colleges/bryn-mawr-college-3237.
63. Higher Education Research Institute at UCLA, "The American Freshman: National Norms Fall 2012," report issued Fall 2012, 4, http://heri.ucla.edu/monographs/TheAmericanFreshman2012.pdf
64. S. D. Lawrence, "Thiel Fellowships Encourage Innovators to Skip College," Online Schools Newsroom, April 22, 2012, http://news.onlineschools.org/2012/04/thiel-fellowships-encourage-innovators-to-skip-college/.

65. Ibid.
66. Ibid.
67. Alan Krueger, "Children Smart Enough to Get into Elite Schools May Not Need to Bother," *New York Times*, April 27, 2000.

Chapter 4: The Lower Side of Higher Ed

1. William James, "The Social Value of the College-Bred," in *The Works of William James: Essays, Comments and Reviews* (Cambridge, MA: Harvard University Press, 1987), 106, emphasis in original, http://books.google.com/books?id=23N0id9Mq3MC&vq=college+education+can+possibly+make&source=gbs_navlinks_s.
2. James, "The True Harvard," in ibid., 76.
3. Philippians 4:8.
4. John Stuart Mill, "Inaugural Address: Delivered to the University of St. Andrews, Feb. 1st 1867" (London: Longmans, Green, 1867), 5, books.google.com/books?id=VxRMAAAAcAAJ.
5. "More on Cortney Munna's Student Loan Tale," *Bucks* (blog), *New York Times*, June 1, 2010, http://bucks.blogs.nytimes.com/2010/06/01/more-on-cortney-munnas-student-loan-saga/.
6. Meghan DeMaria, "Majoring in the Classics Gives Students an Edge," *USA Today*, May 7, 2012, http://www.usatodayeducate.com/staging/index.php/campuslife/opinion-majoring-in-the-classics-gives-students-an-edge.
7. Professor X, "In the Basement of the Ivory Tower," *Atlantic*, June 2008, http://www.theatlantic.com/magazine/archive/2008/06/in-the-basement-of-the-ivory-tower/6810/.
8. Ibid.
9. Ibid.
10. Mary Grigsby, *College Life Through the Eyes of Students* (Albany: State University of New York Press, 2009), 117.

11. Ibid.
12. Daniel de Vise, "Is College Too Easy? As Study Time Falls, Debate Rises," *Washington Post*, May 21, 2012, http://www.washingtonpost.com/local/education/is-college-too-easy-as-study-time-falls-debate-rises/2012/05/21/gIQAp7uUgU_story.html.
13. Stuart Rojstaczer and Christopher Healy, "Where A is Ordinary: The Evolution of American College and University Grading, 1940–2009," *Teachers College Record* 114, no. 7 (2012) http://www.tcrecord.org/content.asp?contentid=16473.
14. Ibid.
15. "Ivy League Grade Inflation," *USA Today*, February 7, 2002, http://www.usatoday.com/news/comment/2002/02/08/edtwof2.htm.
16. Philip Babcock and Mindy Marks, "Leisure College, USA," May 2010, 15, www.econ.ucsb.edu/papers/wp02-10.pdf.
17. Richard Arum and Josipa Roksa, *Academically Adrift* (Chicago: University of Chicago Press, 2011), 98.
18. Babcock and Marks, "Leisure College, USA," 1.
19. Ibid., 5.
20. Arum and Roksa, *Academically Adrift*, 36–37.
21. Cited in Babcock and Marks, "Leisure College, USA," 7.
22. Rebekah Nathan, *My Freshman Year: What a Professor Learned by Becoming a Student* (New York: Penguin Books, 2006), 114. Cited in Arum and Roksa, *Academically Adrift*, 76.
23. "The American College Teacher: National Norms for 2007–2008," Higher Education Research Institute, UCLA, March 2009, http://heri.ucla.edu/PDFs/pubs/briefs/brief-pr030508-08faculty.pdf.
24. R. R. Reno, "Teachers Without Students," *First Things*, June 20, 2011, http://www.firstthings.com/onthesquare/2011/06/teachers-without-students.
25. Mark Bauerlein, "Professors on the Production Line, Students on Their Own," *American Enterprise Institute*

Future of American Education Working Paper, 2009, 5–6, http://www.aei.org/files/1969/12/31/Bauerlein.pdf.

26. Lindsay Waters, "Rescue Tenure from the Tyranny of the Monograph," *Chronicle of Higher Education,* April 20, 2001, http://chronicle.com/article/Rescue-Tenure-From-the-Tyranny/9623.
27. Mark Bauerlein, Mohamed Gad-el-Hak, et al, "We Must Stop the Avalanche of Low-Quality Research," *Chronicle of Higher Education,* June 13, 2010, http://chronicle.com/article/We-Must-Stop-the-Avalanche-of/65890/.
28. Reno, "Teachers."
29. Audrey Williams June, "Professors Seek to Reframe the Salary Debate," *Chronicle of Higher Education,* April 8, 2012, http://chronicle.com/article/faculty-salaries-barely-budge-2012/131432/.
30. Samantha Stainburn, "The Case of the Vanishing Full-Time Professor," *New York Times,* December 30, 2009, http://www.nytimes.com/2010/01/03/education/edlife/03strategy-t.html.
31. Andrew Hacker and Claudia Dreifus, *Higher Education?* (New York: Holt and Company, 2010), 55.
32. Jenna Ashley Robinson, "A Much-Needed Window Into Higher Education," *The Raleigh-Durham Observer,* January 3, 2012, http://www.newsobserver.com/2013/01/03/2581675/a-much-needed-window-into-college.html.
33. High school examination graduation questions, 1895, http://skyways.lib.ks.us/genweb/saline/society/exam.html.
34. Lyndsey Layton and Emma Brown, "SAT Reading Scores Hit a Four-Decade Low," *Washington Post,* September 24, 2012, http://articles.washingtonpost.com/2012-09-24/local/35495510_1_scores-board-president-gaston-caperton-test-takers.
35. Brian Bolduc, "Don't Know Much About History," *Wall Street Journal,* June 18, 2011, http://online.wsj.com/article/SB10001424052702304432304576369421525987128.html.

36. Ibid., emphasis in original.
37. Jennifer Gonzalez, "Lessons Learned, Using Data to Help Students Pass Remedial Courses," April 18, 2012, http://chronicle.com/article/Lessons-Learned-Using-Data-to/65055/.
38. Christine Armario, "Nation Has High College Remedial Education Rate," AP report in *Huffington Post*, May 11, 2010, http://www.huffingtonpost.com/2010/05/11/nation-has-high-college-r_n_571562.html.
39. Ibid.
40. "Remediation: Higher Education's Bridge to Nowhere," Complete College America, April 2012, 2, http://www.completecollege.org/docs/CCA-Remediation-final.pdf.
41. Ibid., 3.
42. Mark Cuban, "The Coming Meltdown in College Education and Why the Economy Won't Get Better Anytime Soon," *Mark Cuban Weblog*, May 12, 2012, http://blogmaverick.com/2012/05/13/the-coming-meltdown-in-college-education-why-the-economy-wont-get-better-any-time-soon/.
43. ACICS, "Survey on Workplace Skills Preparedness," Fact Sheet, November 2011, http://www.acics.org/events/content.aspx?id=4718.
44. Darren Dahl, "A Sea of Job-Seekers, But Some Companies Aren't Getting Any Bites," *New York Times*, June 27, 2012, http://www.nytimes.com/2012/06/28/business/smallbusiness/even-with-high-unemployment-some-small-businesses-struggle-to-fill-positions.html?pagewanted=all.
45. William Bennett, "Why the Chinese Are flocking to U.S. Colleges," CNN.com, May 31, 2012, http://www.cnn.com/2012/05/31/opinion/bennett-china-us-schools/index.html.
46. Peter Berkowitz, "Why Colleges Don't Teach the *Federalist* Papers," *Wall Street Journal*, May 6, 2012, http://online.wsj.com/article/SB10001424052702304743704577380383026226256.html.
47. Leslie Grimard, "The Lady Gaga-fication of Higher

Ed," Heritage Foundation *Foundry* (blog), December 9, 2011, http://blog.heritage.org/2011/12/09/the-lady-gaga-fication-of-higher-ed/.

48. Jason Mattera, "The Dirty Dozen," Townhall.com, December 21, 2006, http://townhall.com/columnists/jasonmattera/2006/12/21/the_dirty_dozen/page/full/.
49. UCLA Office of Undergraduate Admission, "2012–2013 Estimated Undergraduate Student Budget," http://www.admissions.ucla.edu/prospect/budget.htm.
50. American Council of Trustees and Alumni (ACTA), "What Will They Learn? 2009," 2, http://www.goacta.org/publications/what_will_they_learn_2009.
51. Grimard, "The Lady Gaga-fication of Higher Ed."
52. ACTA, "What Will They Learn?" 2.
53. Ibid., 3.
54. Matthew Arnold, *Culture and Anarchy: An Essay in Political and Social Criticism* (London: Smith, Elder, 1869), viii, http://books.google.com/books?id=gVgJAAAAQAAJ&printsec=frontcover&dq=Matthew+Arnold,+Culture+and+Anarchy:+An+Essay+in+Political+and+Social+Criticism&hl=en&sa=X&ei=OR7eUOyJL4nW8gSg8YDICg&ved=0CDoQ6AEwAQ#v=onepage&q=best%20that%20has%20been%20thought%20and%20said&f=false.
55. Harold Rosenberg, *The Tradition of the New* (New York: Da Capo Press, 1994), "The Herd of Independent Minds," part 4 title.
56. The first of the two studies is Daniel Klein and Andrew Western's "Voter Registration of Berkeley and Stanford Faculty," *Academic Questions* 18, no. 1 (Winter 2004–5): 53-65, and the second is Karl Zinsmeister's "The One-Party Campus," which appeared in *AEI* magazine, September 2002. Both studies were compiled into this chart by the National Association of Scholars in the study "A Crisis of Competence: The Corrupting Effect of Political Activism in the University of California," April 2012, http://www

.nas.org/articles/a_crisis_of_competence_the_corrupting_effect_of_political_activism_in_the_u.

57. NAS, "A Crisis of Competence," 20.
58. Ron Meyer, "2012 Commencement Speakers Survey: Liberals Outnumber Conservatives 7:1 at America's Top 100 Universities," Young America's Foundation, *New Guard* (blog), May 14, 2012, http://www.yaf.org/2012_Commencement_Survey.aspx. According to Young America's Foundation, "To qualify as 'liberal' or 'conservative' for the survey, speakers must have publicly supported ideological causes through speaking, writing, serving in public office, commentating, or financial contributions."
59. Stephanie Liu, "99 percent of donors from Princeton give to Obama," The Daily Princetonian, November 6, 2012, http://www.dailyprincetonian.com/2012/11/06/31697.
60. American Council of Trustees and Alumni, "Politics in the Classroom," October–November 2004, https://www.goacta.org/publications/downloads/PoliticsintheClassroom_.pdf. Look under "Reports."
61. "Dozens of UPenn Professors Sign Statement of Solidarity with Occupy Wall St. Protestors," October, 21, 2011, *Daily Pennsylvanian*, http://www.studentsforacademicfreedom.org/news/2835/dozens-of-u-penn-professors-sign-statement-of-solidarity-with-occupy-wall-street-protestors.
62. National Association of Scholars, "Crisis of Competence," 6.
63. Heather MacDonald, "Less Academics, More Narcissism," *City Journal*, July 14, 2011, http://www.city-journal.org/2011/cjc0714hm.html.
64. Jamie Weinstein, "Book: Rise of Gender and Ethnic Studies Programs Helped Bring About Decline of Modern Academia," *Daily Caller*, October 18, 2012, http://dailycaller.com/2012/10/18/book-rise-of-gender-and-ethnic-studies-programs-helped-bring-about-decline-of-modern-academia/.
65. Bruce Bawer, *The Victims' Revolution: The Rise of Identity*

Studies and the Closing of the Liberal Mind (New York: HarperCollins, 2012), 348.

66. George Will, "Colleges Have Free Speech on the Run," *Washington Post*, November 30, 2012, http://www.washingtonpost.com/opinions/george-will-colleges-have-free-speech-on-the-run/2012/11/30/9457072c-3a54-11e2-8a97-363b0f9a0ab3_story.html.
67. Ibid.
68. Greg Toppo, "Students Drink More and More Often if Living in Coed Dorms," *USA Today*, November 17, 2009, http://www.usatoday.com/news/education/2009-11-17-coed17_ST_N.htm.
69. Jeffrey Goldberg, "The Case for More Guns (and More Gun Control)," *Atlantic*, December 2012, http://www.theatlantic.com/magazine/archive/2012/12/the-case-for-more-guns-and-more-gun-control/309161/3/.
70. John Garvey, "Why We're Going Back to Single-Sex Dorms," *Wall Street Journal*, June 13, 2011, http://online.wsj.com/article/SB10001424052702304432304576369843592242356.html.

Chapter 5: With Eyes Wide-Open

1. Kate Brotherton, "25 and Deep in Debt," Cincinnati.com, September 10, 2012, http://news.cincinnati.com/article/20120910/EDIT02/309070142/25-deep-debt.
2. US Department of Education, "Graduation rates of first-time postsecondary students who started as full-time degree/certificate-seeking students, by sex, race/ethnicity, time to completion, and level and control of institution where student started: Selected cohort entry years, 1996 through 2007," *Digest of Education Statistics*, http://nces.ed.gov/programs/digest/d11/tables/dt11_345.asp.
3. Ylan Q. Mui and Suzy Khimm, "College Dropouts Have Debt but No Degree," *Washington Post*, May 28, 2012, http://www.washingtonpost.com/business/economy/college-dropouts-have-debt-but-no-degree/2012/05/28/gJQAnUPqwU_story.html?hpid=z3.

4. Christopher Caldwell, "Live and Let Die," *Claremont Review of Books*, Fall 2012, http://www.claremont.org/publications/crb/id.1970/article_detail.asp.
5. Marty Nemko, "We Send Too Many Students to College," MartyNemko.com, http://www.martynemko.com/articles/we-send-too-many-students-college_id1543.
6. "College Preparedness Lacking, Forcing Students into Developmental Coursework, Forcing Some to Drop Out," *Huffington Post*, June 18, 2012, http://www.huffingtonpost.com/2012/06/18/students-lacking-college-_n_1606201.html.
7. Paul Schmitz, "Lessons from Famous College Dropouts," CNN.com, December 31, 2011, http://www.cnn.com/2011/12/30/opinion/schmitz-college/index.html.
8. Andy Kessler, "Our 19th Century Curriculum," *Weekly Standard*, October 8, 2012, http://www.weeklystandard.com/print/articles/our-19th-century-curriculum_653241.html.
9. David Brooks, "The Missing Fifth," *New York Times*, May 9, 2011, http://www.nytimes.com/2011/05/10/opinion/10brooks.html.
10. Robert Schwartz et al., "Pathways to Prosperity," February 2011, 7, https://docs.google.com/viewer?a=v&q=cache:7RetBCMGlxwJ:www.gse.harvard.edu/news_events/features/2011/Pathways_to_Prosperity_Feb2011.pdf+%22narrowly+defined+'college+for+all'+goal&hl=en&gl=us&pid=bl&srcid=ADGEESgKH-2wVXxGA8rAmde6b-pzS2xtzu0dClfCPO6f854jIKY7qnqZavviXdVhLfBvGcUHvXl_pZklKXyGAVKDyC1b09_-p2HUsVE3nl1ax-dFYLl03PI3CRsLt1D6EqYBkT5oKICM&sig=AHIEtbT2E8bvjI7PskvK56vxIP61Z9RwUw.
11. Robert Samuelson, "It's Time to Drop the College-for-All Crusade," *Washington Post*, May 27, 2012, http://www.washingtonpost.com/opinions/its-time-to-drop-the-college-for-all-crusade/2012/05/27/gJQAzcUGvU_print.html.
12. Lorraine Woellert, "Companies Say 3 Million Unfilled Positions in Skills Crisis," Bloomberg.com, July 24, 2012,

http://www.bloomberg.com/news/2012-07-25/companies-say-3-million-unfilled-positions-in-skill-crisis-jobs.html.

13. Valerie Strauss, "Bring Back Shop Class," *Washington Post*, December 22, 2010, http://voices.washingtonpost.com/answer-sheet/guest-bloggers/bring-back-shop-class.html.
14. "A Conversation with Senators Wyden and Rubio: Holding Higher Education Accountable," comments delivered at the American Enterprise Institute, September 19, 2012, http://www.aei.org/events/2012/09/19/a-conversation-with-senator-wyden-and-senator-rubio-holding-higher-education-accountable/.
15. Melissa Korn, "Is An Ivy League Degree Worth It?" *Wall Street Journal*, November 8, 2011, http://online.wsj.com/article/SB10001424052970203733504577023892064201700.html.
16. Ibid.
17. Harvard Law School, "Undergraduate Colleges," http://www.law.harvard.edu/prospective/jd/apply/undergrads.html.
18. Joe Richter, "Harvard Losing Out to South Dakota in Graduate Pay: Commodities," *Bloomberg News*, September 18, 2012, http://www.bloomberg.com/news/2012-09-17/harvard-losing-out-to-south-dakota-in-graduate-pay-commodities.html.
19. Matt Schifrin, "Lessons from a Master Marketer," *Forbes*, January 17, 2011, http://www.forbes.com/forbes/2011/0117/entrepreneurs-brandon-hidalgo-dvds-marketing-master-class.html.
20. Mitch Smith, "Old School Becomes New School," *Inside Higher Ed*, April 17, 2012, http://www.insidehighered.com/news/2012/04/17/new-york-project-seeks-wider-audience-liberal-arts.
21. "Georgetown University Offers College Course on Jay-Z," FoxNews.com, December 3, 2011, http://www.foxnews.com/us/2011/12/03/georgetown-university-offers-college-course-on-jay-z/.
22. John Gravois, "The College For-Profits Should Fear,"

Washington Monthly, September–October 2011, http://www.washingtonmonthly.com/magazine/septemberoctober_2011/features/the_college_forprofits_should031640.php.

23. Nate Hindman, "E[nstitute] School for Entrepreneurs, Emerges from New York Startup Scene," *Huffington Post*, April 4, 2012, http://www.huffingtonpost.com/2012/04/04/enstitute-a-school-for-entrepreneurs_n_1403036.html; http://enstituteu.com/.
24. Annie Murphy Paul, "School of Hard Knocks," *New York Times*, August 23, 2012, http://www.nytimes.com/2012/08/26/books/review/how-children-succeed-by-paul-tough.html?pagewanted=all&_r=0.
25. Judy Bolton-Fasman, "How Children Succeed: An Interview with Paul Tough," *Huffington Post*, September 21, 2012, http://www.huffingtonpost.com/judy-boltonfasman/paul-tough_b_1903320.html.
26. Shirley Jinkins, "Area Educators Team Up to Offer $10,000 Bachelor's Degree," *Ft. Worth Star-Telegram*, July 26, 2012, http://www.star-telegram.com/2012/07/25/4126529/area-educators-team-up-to-offer.html.
27. Kaustuv Basu, "The Radical New Humanities Ph.D," *Inside Higher Ed*, May 16, 2012, http://www.insidehighered.com/news/2012/05/16/rethinking-humanities-phd.
28. Ibid.
29. David Brooks, "The Campus Tsunami," *New York Times*, May 3, 2012, http://www.nytimes.com/2012/05/04/opinion/brooks-the-campus-tsunami.html?_r=2.
30. Nick DeSantis, "A Boom Time for Education Start-Ups," *Chronicle of Higher Education*, March 18, 2012, http://chronicle.com/article/A-Boom-Time-for-Education/131229/.
31. John Chubb and Terry Moe, "Higher Education's Online Revolution," *Wall Street Journal*, May 30, 2012, http://online.wsj.com/article/SB10001424052702304019404577416631206583286.html.
32. Daniel Luzer, "Who Runs the University of Virginia?"

Washington Monthly, June 18, 2012, http://www.washingtonmonthly.com/college_guide/blog/who_runs_the_university_of_vir.php?page=all.

33. Brooks, "Campus Tsunami."
34. Ken Auletta, "Get Rich U," *New Yorker*, April 30, 2012, http://www.newyorker.com/reporting/2012/04/30/120430fa_fact_auletta.
35. Bill is a member of Udacity's Advisory Board.
36. Adam Falk, "In Defense of the Living, Breathing Professor," *Wall Street Journal*, August 28, 2012, http://online.wsj.com/article/SB1000087239639044432720457761559274679990 0.html.
37. Jeffrey R. Young, "Dozens of Plagiarism Incidents Are Reported in Coursera's Free Online Courses," *Chronicle of Higher Education*, August 16, 2012, http://chronicle.com/article/Dozens-of-Plagiarism-Incidents/133697/.

Index

P

Q

R

S